Diamond Clear Friendly Beer
The Grain Belt Story

An illustrated history by Jeff R. Lonto

STUDIO Z-7 PUBLISHING
MINNEAPOLIS, MINNESOTA
www.studioZ7.com

© 2019 by Jeff R. Lonto. All rights reserved. No part of this book may be reproduced in any manner without the written permission of the author except in the case of brief quotations embodied in critical articles and reviews.

Printed in the United States of America.

Published by Studio Z-7 Publishing
813 Marshall Street NE
Minneapolis, MN 55413-1816
www.studioz7.com

Cover design and layout by Jeff R. Lonto

Grain Belt and associated trademarks are owned by August Schell Brewing Company, New Ulm, Minnesota. This publication is not officially authorized by August Schell Brewing Company and the opinions expressed are solely those of the author.

Contents

Introduction……………………………………………………………………2

The Early Years………………………………………………………………6

Prohibition……………………………………………………………………18

Roll Out The Barrel…………………………………………………………21

It's Been a Long Time a-Brewing………………………………………34

Welcome To Grain Belt Park………………………………………………48

The Fountain Runs Dry……………………………………………………66

House of Heileman…………………………………………………………71

Minnesota Brewing Company……………………………………………78

Grain Belt Moves to New Ulm……………………………………………88

A few extras…………………………………………………………………102

About the author……………………………………………………………104

Introduction

From the 1890s until the mid-1970s, the Grain Belt Brewery was the heartbeat of the Northeast Minneapolis neighborhood where it sat, and the focal point of the community. It was one of the neighborhood's biggest employers, it produced the best selling beer in the state, it was at one point the 18th largest brewer in the country, and it was a popular tourist attraction, especially after the scenic park was opened outside the Broadway Avenue side of the brewery in the early 1960s. But in 1975, a local businessman took it over and essentially ran it into the ground. The following year 350 jobs were gone, the equipment was auctioned off mostly for scrap, and the buildings were boarded up, with the possibility of demolition looming.

The Grain Belt brand, and the abandoned brewery itself held so much lore and mystique for me personally from childhood on. In 1993 I moved in to a house just a few blocks away from the historic castle-like brewery that took up an entire city block in Northeast Minneapolis. At the time, the brewery was dark and boarded up, having last operated some eighteen years earlier. The little Grain Belt Park in front, however, was still pretty much in tact. A pipe stuck out of the ground where the famous "Diamond Wells" Fountain once flowed, the wooden benches and landscaping were still there, and the grass was kept mowed.

My fascination with Grain Belt dated back to when I was a young child living in an apartment building in a Minneapolis suburb, where my bedroom window happened to face a big billboard that displayed eye-catching 24-sheet posters advertising Grain Belt beer that would change about once a month. I was particularly in awe at seeing men out there posting a new ad, one sheet at a time, over the old one. From there, I started drawing my own Grain Belt posters with my crayons and paper. When we were learning about ecology in kindergarten and we had to draw pictures depicting pollution, I drew a man throwing Grain Belt cans into a lake. My young female teacher actually liked it.

Grain Belt was the dominant beer brand in Minnesota, the beer that most of my relatives and their friends drank, and along with the

The Grain Belt Brewery in 1993.

humorous, eye-catching billboards around the city and highways, red and gold Grain Belt signs were easily spotted outside of bars and corner stores. I had also heard stories about what a fun brewery tour it was, but never got to take one.

Eventually, somebody had given me a pamphlet called "Welcome to Grain Belt," which had full color pictures of the brewery and products on the outside, with a history of Grain Belt and a diagram of how beer is made on the inside. It got me interested enough in the brewery to pay attention to news reports about the intentions of property owner Irwin Jacobs to tear it down, and the effort of local historians and community activists to save it from destruction. All this was happening just as the beer can collecting craze with young guys was catching on, and I was completely into that.

Grain Belt pamphlet from the 1970s.

Against the odds, the brewery was saved. By the time I moved into the neighborhood, the ownership of the property had been transferred to the Minneapolis Community Development Agency. Demolition wasn't entirely off the table, but it was far less inevitable.

In 1998, I published a book about Grain Belt called "Legend of the Brewery, a Brief History of the Minneapolis Brewing Heritage." That publication led me to an invitation to be part of a community tour of the brewery, conducted by the Minneapolis Community Development Agency. On September 8, 1999, I finally got to see the inside of the thing, after all the dreams I had had about walking in there and seeing some kind of holy grail.

Going in through a back door, one of the first things noticeable was a musty basement smell. Apparently that was due in part to yeast residue still in the building from the brewing days. An ornamental iron staircase from the frilly Victorian era wound its way through the building, painted in an industrial green, as were the walls. There were strange, obscure rooms, some with narrow doorways about two feet wide. A large "Grain Belt Guys" billboard, from the company's last ad campaign in 1975, was on a wall in the old engine room, and a red Grain Belt logo was still painted on a wall in the old brewery laboratory, although it was chipping away.

A few pieces of equipment remained, such as original 470-bbl fermenting tanks made of stainless steel, and some old machinery, though most of the original equipment was auctioned off for scrap back in 1976. In fact, there were giant holes in the floor where the copper brew

A few interior shots the Grain Belt brewery in 1999, almost a quarter century after it closed, and just before big renovations happened.

kettles used to be.

Some of the rooms had lighting from bulbs strung across, others were completely dark, and we were all given flashlights to use. Graffiti could be found here and there, including a mysterious recipe for "Quick Tuna Hotdish" written on a wall. Remains of a shower stall were adjacent to the rest rooms, and although the plumbing had been shut off back in 1976, that didn't stop a few intruders over the years from using the toilets.

We even got to go out on the roof of the brewery on that warm September morning and see the incredible views of the neighborhood and downtown Minneapolis. We walked out to the glass atrium atop one of the building sections, which housed an observation deck. Beyond the rails around the catwalks, one could see all the way down to the bottom floor, with the ornamental iron staircase winding its way around. Ever have a falling dream?

Since then, much has happened at the old brewery as well as with the marketing of Grain Belt beer. This book serves as a successor to my 1998 book, "Legend of the Brewery," expanded and updated.

Jeff R. Lonto
July 2019

The Early Years

Minneapolis was a growing, thriving urban center in the middle to late nineteenth century. Built around the banks of the Mississippi River, they young city grew on the lumber and flour milling industries. With its connection to the river, and as a major railroad hub, Minneapolis quickly became the central market for grains grown throughout the Midwest. Settlers of German descent were among those who made Minnesota their home. The German influence and the ready access to the state's plentiful barley crop made brewing another one of Minnesota's boom industries.

It was a logical choice for the brewing industry to locate and grow. It was said that the world's best malting barley came from the Red River Valley of the North, with its agricultural richness. The region's first brewery was established by Anthony Yoerg in 1848, one year before the founding of Minnesota Territory, in St. Paul. (Minnesota would not become a state until 1858.) The Yoerg Brewery remained in business for just over a century.

Minnesota's second brewery was started by a French immigrant named John Orth in 1850 near what would become the site of the Grain Belt Brewery, near the Mississippi River. Born in 1821 in the Alsace region of France, Orth immigrated to America in 1849, settling in the village of St. Anthony. He established his brewery on the East Bank of the river, using caves at nearby Nicollet Island to store his product.

John Orth's first name was misspelled in this mid-19th Century illustration of his brewery in Minneapolis.

1889 Minneapolis City Directory ad.

The following ad ran in the December 17, 1850 edition of the Minnesota Democrat newspaper:

MINNESOTA BREWERY, AT ST. ANTHONY FALLS

--I am now ready to supply the citizens of this Territory with Ale and Beer, which will be found to be equal--yes, superior--to what is brought from below. I am now demonstrating that malt liquors of the very best quality can be manufactured in Minnesota. Try my Ale and Beer and you will be convinced of the fact.

JOHN ORTH

Seven years after the Orth Brewery was established, Gottlieb Gluek built his brewery just up the street. By 1890, there were over 100 breweries operating in Minnesota.

In addition to running his brewery, John Orth was elected to the first St. Anthony City Council in 1855 and to the first City Council when St. Anthony and Minneapolis merged in 1872. A supporter of the anti-slavery movement, Orth was an active member of Lincoln's Republican Party. He switched to the Democrats later in life, however, as the Republicans of the time were becoming more and more sympathetic to the growing prohibition movement.

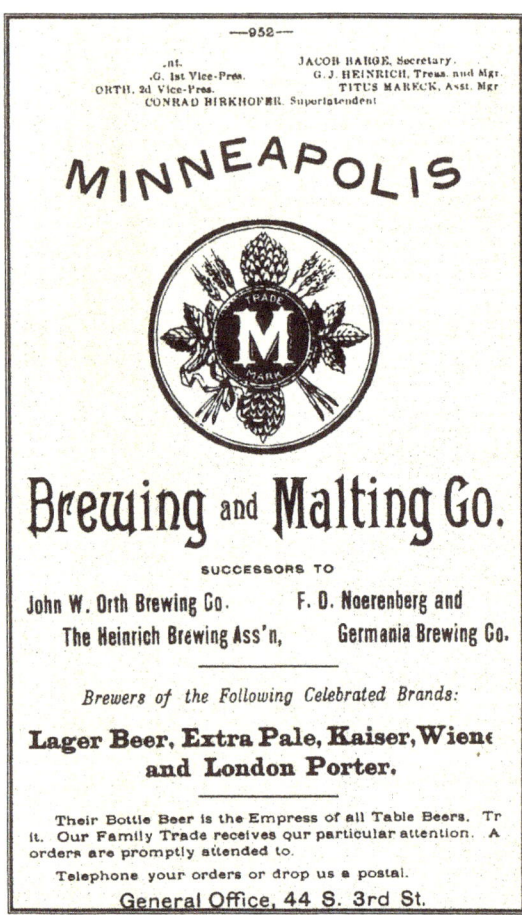

Minneapolis City Directory ad from 1891, announcing the formation of the Minneapolis Brewing and Malting Company.

As the cities of Minneapolis and St. Paul grew, other breweries were popping up and the competition was fierce. In what is often called the "Gilded Age" and the time of the Industrial Revolution, there was actually something of a depression in the final decade of the nineteenth century. The economy was unstable, resulting in anxiety in many industries, including brewing, that lead to merger mania.

It is perhaps this that led Orth to consolidating his brewing company with three other Minneapolis brewers: the Heinrich Brewing Association, F.D. Norenberg Brewing & Malt House, and Germainia Brewing Association, to form the Minneapolis Brewing and Malting Company, officially incorporated on July 15, 1890. Minneapolis brewer Gottlieb Gluek was invited to be part of this merger, but he chose to stay independent.

With the formulation of the new company, primary headquarters was at the Orth Brewery, although beer continued to be produced at the Heinrich and Germania plants as well, with the company business office in downtown Minneapolis on First Avenue, next to the main post office. For the company to remain competitive, however, it was realized that production needed to be consolidated in one high-volume facility to produce at least 150,000 barrels of beer a year.

The New, Modern Brewery

A new brewery was constructed near the Orth site, at 1215 Marshall Street Northeast, beginning in 1890. Production began at the new facility in 1892. The new Minneapolis Brewing and Malting Company complex consisted of a massive brewhouse, bottling houses, a warehouse and stables for the horses that pulled the delivery wagons. Some of the buildings were left over from the Orth Brewery. The site included access to the river and railroad tracks. The brewhouse was designed with four different sections built together, which some say symbolized the four companies that formed the Minneapolis Brewing and Malting Company.

Considered at the time to be one of the largest and most modern brewing facilities in the country, its initial cost was $500,000 with a production capacity of 300,000 barrels annually. Additions over the next decade brought production up to a half-million barrels per year. The wooden barrels and glass bottles of beer were transported from the brewery in horse-drawn wagons. Early brands had such names as Gilt Edge, Wiener, Kaiser, London Porter and Extra Pale.

In 1893, the company was reorganized, and the name was shortened to Minneapolis Brewing Company. It was in that year that the company introduced Golden Grain Belt Old Lager to the market. Early Grain Belt labels illustrated a golden barley field beneath blue skies inside the now-familiar diamond logo, and assured customers that the beer was "Properly sterilized--Does not cause biliousness," the excess production of stomach bile.

The name "Grain Belt" referred to the geographical area of the country where the beer was brewed. The South had the Cotton Belt and the North had the Grain Belt. The brand caught the public fancy and it soon became the flagship brand of the Minneapolis Brewing Company. Other brews made by the company, such as Gilt Edge and London Porter, adopted diamond-shaped labels and were advertised collectively as "The Golden Grain Belt Beers."

Early beer bottles were embossed with the words 'THIS BOTTLE NOT TO BE SOLD"

The Minneapolis Brewing and Malting Company, seen from the northeast corner in this circa 1892 depiction.

"Golden Grain Belt Old Lager" was introduced in 1893.

which simply meant the bottle was property of the brewery and couldn't be used for other things for sale. Labels were not required to list the net weight until the passage of the historic Pure Food and Drug Act of 1906.

Getting bottled beer from the brewery to the consumer was simpler in those pre-Prohibition days. One could simply contact the brewery and have them deliver a case to the customer's home. No middle man distributors then.

However, about 75 percent of the beer produced by Minneapolis Brewing Company at the time was not sold in bottles, but from wooden barrels that were made right at the brewery, and tapped by saloons that generally sold beer for five cents a glass. Many of the saloons, known as tied houses, were owned by the brewery and sold only Minneapolis Brewing Company products, a practice used throughout the industry at the time.

The Great Fire of 1893

But the company, as well as a large part of the city, suffered major losses the same year that Grain Belt was introduced. On August 13, 1893, a Sunday afternoon, fire broke out at a stable located at Nicollet Island, on the Mississippi River. As firemen battled the blaze, an incendiary hit some lumber being stored on nearby Boom Island and the fire spread rapidly through Northeast Minneapolis, taking numerous homes, mills, lumber yards and factories with it. It was the most devastating fire in the city's history at the time.

The inferno burned several city blocks, making its way to the Minneapolis Brewing Company complex, destroying a malt house, three bottling houses, a pitch yard and a barn (as this was in the days when deliveries were made by horse-drawn wagons). There was only minimal damage to the main brewhouse, however, due to its fire-resistant structure and a wind shift. The company's loss was reported to be $117,000.

The buildings were fully insured and the company took the time to rebuild and expand. In 1904, an

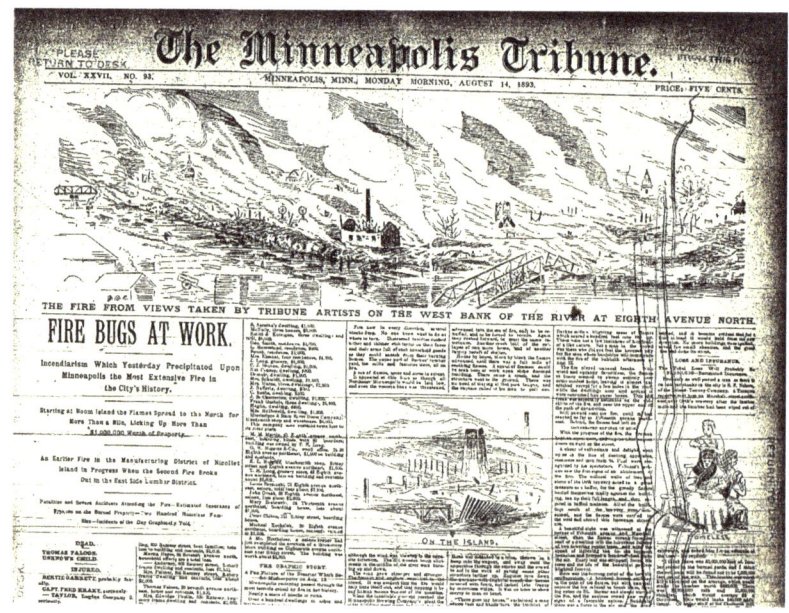

Front page of the Minneapolis Tribune from August 14, 1893 about the Northeast Minneapolis fires.

addition was built on the south end of the brewhouse and a new, much larger bottling house and warehouse were built along 13th Avenue Northeast, across from the north side of the brewhouse. Soon, the complex became something of a small village with its own paint shop, wagon shot, machine shop and carpenter shop. The "village" was said to be worth $1.1 million in 1910.

Moving Into a New Century

The Minneapolis Brewing Company continued to expand and grow as Minnesota entered the twentieth century. It quickly became one of the largest beer producers in the state, second only to the Theodore Hamm Brewing Company in St. Paul. Although rivals, Hamm and Minneapolis Brewing joined forces in 1904 and built a cold storage unit in Kittson County in northwestern Minnesota for their mutual usage, to counter expansion into the state by G. Heileman Brewing Company of La Crosse, Wisconsin.

Horses were a big part of the operation at Minneapolis Brewing Company in the late 1890s and early 1900s. As a retrospective article in the January 1956 issue of the Grain Belt Diamond, a company magazine, described, "In the early days, the heavy draft horses were pointed to with pride by the Minneapolis Brewing Company. Kids throughout

Detail from a turn-of-the-century poster.

the city hitched their sleds to Grain Belt wagons. Company men groomed their horses meticulously with a spirit of competition with other breweries.

"Usually, each brewery had an exclusive on the color of their horses. The Minneapolis Brewing Company had blacks. Other companies used greys, sorrels and bays."

From 1910 to 1915 the company hosted "Grain Belt Week" during the summer, where the public was invited to meet at the old company offices in downtown Minneapolis and were driven out to the brewery where they were given a tour and were treated to lunch and all the beer they wanted, according to an article in the March 1956 Grain Belt Diamond.

In 1912, the expanding Minneapolis Brewing Company moved out of its rented downtown Minneapolis offices on First Avenue next to the post office, building its own offices across from the brewery on Marshall Street Northeast.

The Minneapolis Tribune on March 31, 1912 reported, "The move was made imperative because of the large business increase, and need for more room...Those who have seen it

Sheet music for "Zum-Zum-Zum: A Stein Song," published in 1914 by Minneapolis Brewing Company to promote Zumalweiss beer.

assert that it is the handsomest and most complete office accommodations in the city, and no concern of the same kind in the northwest boasts of such handsome accommodations...

"An especially new feature in the new offices is the sanitary provision, which argues for good health among employes [sic]. Such care has been taken with modern ideas of sanitary office buildings that all employes [sic] have conditions as healthful as if they were working out of doors."

Minneapolis Brewing Company promoted its products in a number of different ways. Some early ads featured paintings of wholesome-looking, wide-eyed Victorian women to counter the saloon image. For the saloon crowd, the company promoted its Zumalweiss beer with "Zum-Zum-Zum: A Stein Song" that could be sung while beering away the hours by the old piano. Kind of a precursor to the radio and television commercial jingles of decades later. The song was available as sheet music, and a recorded version on a 78 r.p.m. record.

Other ads promoted Zumalweiss, Grain Belt and other beers as a "family beverage" and promising it to be "a perfect tonic promoting restful sleep and aiding appetite."

Minneapolis Brewing Company expanded its market widely in that first decade of the century, conducting business in Minnesota, Wisconsin, North Dakota, South Dakota (the Dakotas actually entered the union as dry states), Iowa, Nebraska, Montana, Illinois and Michigan. In 1914, beer consumption in the United States reached an all-time high of 66 million barrels.

But in addition to all the beer, the Prohibition Movement was brewing. The movement was rapidly gaining momentum and political clout, making life difficult for brewers, distillers and saloon owners.

With the ratification of the 18th Amendment to the United States Constitution, National Prohibition took hold on January 16, 1920 and Grain Belt beer became illegal.

A rare inside view of the Minneapolis Brewing Company brewery, circa 1898.

ASSEMBLY LINE—Keg house operations have changed at Minneapolis Brewing Co. since this picture was snapped in the late 19th century.

FILL 'ER UP—Filling and capping operations are a far cry from the modern equipment now being installed in the bottlehouse as part of the Grain Belt modernization program.

Keg House and Bottle House operations at the Minneapolis Brewing Company in the 1890s, from a retrospective article in the January 1956 issue of the Grain Belt Diamond, a company magazine.

Grain Belt products were promoted as "The Beers of Society" on the cover of the 1897 edition of Dual City Blue Book, an old city directory aimed at the upper crust.

These distinguished gentlemen will drink to that!

DRIVER-HELPER—Golden Grain Belt beers reached as far as a team of horses could travel, but the competitive spirit made up for the lack of distance. Here, a photo taken in the late 1890's, shows how beer was delivered. Pride in the old percheron draft horses was the keynote of the era.

Horse-drawn Grain Belt beer wagon, pictured in a retrospective article in the January 1956 issue of the Grain Belt Diamond, a company magazine.

Turn-of-the-century Grain Belt warehouse, location unknown, from the Grain Belt Diamond, October 1965.

The brewery was depicted in this 1895 ad for Gilt Edge Beer, from Dual City Blue Book.

Ad from the St. Paul Pioneer Press, November 9, 1899.

1890s lithograph advertising Minneapolis Brewing Company's Bock beer, featuring two goats pulling a maiden through a grain field.

To counter the Temperance Movement, health claims were made in this baseball-themed Grain Belt newspaper ad from 1910. Sports sections were often in pink to stand out from the rest of the paper.

Some pre-Prohibition Minneapolis Brewing Company bottles.

Minneapolis Brewing Company ceramic mugs from the 1890s.

Prohibition

As America entered the Twentieth Century, times and attitudes were rapidly changing. With the new century there was a fresh sense of optimism, times were good and the industrial revolution was well under way. We'd be on the road to a nearly perfect society, some felt, if only the evils of demon liquor were eliminated.

The movement to prohibit alcoholic beverages had been bubbling for decades. It started from the pulpits of the Protestant churches which dotted the Midwestern frontier throughout the Nineteenth Century. It was this religious fervor that became the backbone of such organizations as the Women's Christian Temperance Union and the Anti-Saloon League, which would slowly but gradually gain public support and political clout.

Crime, domestic abuse and disease were blamed on the seductive forces of alcohol. Saloons were seen as places were despicable men gathered to spit, swear and fight, not to mention get drunk, often abusing or abandoning innocent wives and children as a result.

The prohibition movement was spawned in the puritan Midwest and Minnesota played a major role in it. As early as 1852, the Minnesota Territorial Legislature briefly enacted a Prohibition law, only to have it struck down by the Territorial Supreme Court. There were numerous attempts to enact laws prohibiting or severely restricting the sale and manufacture of alcoholic beverages. The most serious of such attempts came with the passage of the Minnesota County Options Law.

The County Options Law, enacted in 1915, allowed counties to go dry by referendum. Popular sentiment was turning in favor of the prohibitionists and by July of that year, 46 counties had approved option referendums out of 51 attempts. In response, Minneapolis Brewing Company started a subsidiary, the Golden Grain Juice Company, in the business of "the manufacture of, and the buying and dealing in non-intoxicating beverages."

Brewers found themselves particularly in the hot seat of the prohibition debate as the United States entered World War I. Strong anti-German hysteria had swept the nation, often to the point of turning ugly. Beer was the beverage of the Germans and companies such as Minneapolis Brewing had executives with names such as Heinrich and Kunz. The more gullible and/or hate mongering members of the public saw these hard working American citizens as The Enemy.

Ultimately it was a Minnesota Congressman named Andrew J. Volstead who would push the hardest for national prohibition. The Volstead Act was the Enforcement Arm of the 18th

Amendment to the United States Constitution. Effective January 16, 1920, the "Noble Experiment" began. The entire nation was officially dry.

Golden Grain Juice Company

Breweries across the country tried staying in business by diversifying into other product lines. Soft drinks, candy, cheese and non-alcoholic malt beverages were among the goods being manufactured by former brewers. When National Prohibition took hold, Golden Grain Juice Company was the vehicle with which Minneapolis Brewing would attempt to survive.

Golden Grain Juice Company's primary product was near beer, a malt beverage with no more than 0.5 percent of alcohol. A 90-foot still was built in the brewhouse, which included a de-alcoholizing unit. Made like regular beer, the brew was boiled down in the still, with the alcohol extracted and stored in tanks under government seal.

Minneapolis City Directory ad for Golden Grain Juice Company, 1925.

The near beer was marketed primarily under the name Minnehaha Pale. Minneapolis Brewing had previously made a Minnehaha Ale. The Golden Grain Juice Company also marketed soft drinks and juices.

Sales were promising at first but they quickly began to slide. In spite of federal law, real beer and spirits were readily available through bootlegging or to anyone who took the time to make it themselves.

With the near beer production, there was the question of what to do with the extracted alcohol that was being stored in the locked tanks that were taking up space in the brewery. To solve this problem, the Kunz Preparations Company was formed, named after Minneapolis Brewing general manager Jacob Kunz. The extracted alcohol was manufactured into rubbing alcohols, toilet preparations and barber's supplies under the Koonz brand name. But the government even discouraged this use of alcohol, charging a $5,000 fee just to apply for a permit. There were also

Zumalweiss made a brief comeback as a near beer in 1927.

Canadian Grain Belt

Meanwhile, Grain Belt beer turned up in Canada. Canadian brewery historian Bill Wright explains that during Prohibition in the US, Charles and Thomas Kiewel, who built the Kiewel brewery in Little Falls, Minnesota, came to St. Boniface, Manitoba to build a new brewery in 1925. There was a trade mark challenge to one of their brands, called Buffalo beer, so the brand was changed to Grain Belt. Canadian Grain Belt was a dark, full-bodied beer, much different from what Minneapolis Grain Belt was known for. Canadian Grain Belt's label design was similar to Minneapolis Grain Belt, including a diamond logo.

Canadian Grain Belt beer label from the Kiewel Brewing Company, Ltd. of St. Boniface, Manitoba.

Riding Out Prohibition

Minneapolis Brewing Company officials had hoped that Prohibition wouldn't last but by the end of the 1920s, with repeal nowhere in sight, company officers conceded that the company couldn't continue. In October 1929, a liquidation dividend of $5 per share was paid to stockholders. Officers' salaries were reduced and company president Fredrich D. Noerenberg's salary was eliminated. Zumalweiss, Minnehaha Pale and a few other minor brands were sold to the Theodore Hamm Brewing Company of St. Paul.

In an attempt to bring in some cash flow, the company leased space in the bottling house to the Minneapolis Standard Garage Company to store automobiles – seized by the Treasury Department's Bureau of Prohibition – at $2.50 per car per month.

The brewhouse on Marshall Street remained idle and was almost sold in 1933. But popular sentiment was changing. It became all too clear that the Noble Experiment was failing. Booze was readily available to anyone who really wanted it, making numerous average citizens outlaws and with the profiteering from the illegal trade of alcoholic beverages, crime rates skyrocketed.

Finally on April 7, 1933, the 21st Amendment to the United States Constitution was ratified by enough states to repeal National Prohibition after thirteen years. Old Man Beer was back.

Roll Out The Barrel

Minnesota did not ratify the 21st Amendment until January 6, 1934 so it officially remained a "dry" state. Strong beer and liquor could not be sold but the federal standard for non-intoxicating malt beverages had recently been redefined through the Cullen Act of 1933, allowing the production of beer not exceeding 3.2 percent of alcohol by weight, up from the 0.5 near beer standard. Minnesota brewers could resume production of "three-two" beer, although many counties chose to remain totally dry.

The brewery had been idle since 1929 so Minneapolis Brewing Company needed to raise capital for badly needed renovations. In its financial desperation in the latter years of Prohibition, the company sold off many of its assets, including its on-site warehouse, which was sold in 1930 for $24,000. Knowing how important it was for the company to have it back, the new owner offered it for $60,000. The company reluctantly settled for $50,000.

In an open letter to the public, Jacob Kunz, now president of the reorganized Minneapolis Brewing Company, promised that the "Golden Grain Belt Beers" that were so fondly remembered would soon be back on the market. The main brewhouse was thoroughly cleaned up, which included sandblasting the entire building inside and out (ultimately causing some damage to the building). New equipment was purchased and the brewing process began. But it would be several months before any beer would be ready for sale to the public. Meanwhile, the other big Twin Cities brewers, Gluek, Hamm and Schmidt, had product ready to go on April 7, 1933, the day of Repeal.

Finally in October 1933, Minneapolis Brewing Company began rolling out barrels of draft beer and on December 14, bottled beer. While it had marketed a number of different brands

Newspaper ad announcing the coming return of Grain Belt beer in bottles on December, 14, 1933.

Full-page ad in the Minneapolis Tribune, December 14, 1933.

in the past, primary emphasis would now be on the Grain Belt label, which had been its most popular brand before Prohibition. It was soon promoted in newspaper ads as "The Friendly Beer." The company also brewed Canterbury Ale, available on tap only.

Even with repeal, there were plenty of arbitrary regulations placed on the brewing and distilling industries by states and local municipalities and the "drys" did everything they could to harass the revived businesses.

In 1933, just as Minneapolis Brewing Company resumed operations, the old prohibitionists attempted to shut it down using a city ordinance prohibiting the sale and production of alcoholic beverages. The city repealed the ordinance soon after the rest of the country but the prohibitionists tried again a few years later as the assistant city attorney, Joseph Hadley, head of the Hennepin County branch of the Minnesota Temperance Movement, filed a complaint in municipal court against Minneapolis Brewing on May 22, 1936, charging the company with owning equipment and having interest in a local tavern, contrary to city ordinance. Similar charges mentioning another tavern were brought two months later.

The complaint said that the brewery's alleged actions were "against the peace and dignity of the State of Minnesota. Wherefore, complainant prays that said offender may be arrested and dealt with according to law."

His prayers were not answered. Municipal Judge Fred B. Wright dismissed the charges the following March, on the grounds that the complaints were insufficient and not specific enough. There was no getting around it, beer was here to stay.

Grain Belt bottle label, circa 1933-34.

The Brewery Bounces Back

Rehabilitation of the brewery was completed in the spring of 1934. Company vice president Charles Kiewel (one of the men who brought Grain Belt beer to Canada during Prohibition), reported to the Board of Directors that 65-70,000 barrels of beer were being brewed in "anticipation of a good summer." Post-Prohibition demand was so high that delivery trucks stayed out twelve to fifteen hours a day just to keep up. Minneapolis Brewing Company sold 30,000 barrels in June 1934 alone, generating profit in excess of $19,000 for the month. By the end of the decade, Grain Belt beer was being marketed in as many as twenty states and the company was employing about 600 workers at the Minneapolis plant.

It was the time of the Great Depression and there was no shortage of workers to bring into the breweries to keep up with the demand. Minneapolis Brewing Company further upgraded and

Snapshot of the Minneapolis Brewing Company brewery in the 1930s.

expanded its facilities.

With these upgrades, in 1934 the company opened a tap room in the basement of its office building across the street from the brewery. Named "The Friendship Room," it was used for company functions as well as meetings "for bona fide organizations regardless of race, religion or creed throughout the year."

Draft horses pulling beer wagons were long gone. There were now a fleet of Grain Belt trucks making deliveries throughout the city and state on paved roads. Kegs were now made of metal rather than wood. Taverns owned by the brewery were a thing of the past as well.

The business of brewing and consumer preferences had changed since the days before Prohibition. More beer was being consumed at home instead of in the taverns, a result of electric refrigerators becoming present in an increasing number of homes, and because of beer drinkers' loss of the "tavern habit." Consequently, bottled beer was far outselling tap beer. New packaging was developed to meet the new demands.

Grain Belt newspaper ad from November 12, 1935, also mentioning the availability of Canterbury Ale on draft.

New Packaging

Until 1935, all packaged beer was available in long-neck bottles that required the purchaser to pay a small deposit and then return the empties to the store where the deposit would be refunded and the bottles ultimately returned to the brewery where they would be washed and refilled.

But in January of that year, the American Can Company convinced the G. Krueger Brewing Company of Newark, NJ to sell its beer in throwaway metal cans that were opened with a special punch-type opener that was given away with purchase. The concept was surprisingly popular, and soon other breweries were offering beer in cans.

Meanwhile, competing manufacturer Continental Can Company came up with its own metal container for beer, with a sloping top often referred to as a cone top, sealed with a regular bottle cap that could be opened with any standard bottle opener.

Not to be outdone, the glass industry innovated its own "stubby" throwaway bottle, with a height and diameter similar to cans, for the legions of beer drinkers who liked the convenience of non-returnable packaging but thought beer was superior in bottles.

Minneapolis Brewing Company considered all of this by polling its consumers in newspaper ads that appeared in October 1935 asking which style of can they would prefer for Grain Belt beer. A few weeks later, the company, citing overwhelming response, announced Grain Belt would soon be available in cap-sealed cans as well as stubby non-returnable bottles, along with traditional long-neck returnable bottles. All those packages held the same amount of beer, 12 fluid ounces. Grain Belt also marketed beer in quart bottles, and large half-gallon "picnic bottles" of unpasteurized "keg beer," with a label that had a depiction of the Minneapolis brewery. They were called picnic bottles because they were often brought along to serve at picnics. However, it was the stubby or "Stein" bottle as the brewery called it, that was most promoted in 1930s advertising. Most Grain Belt bottles were brown (amber) at the time.

Newspaper ad from October 23, 1935 asked the public to decide which style of beer can Grain Belt should come in, Cap-Sealed (cone top) or flat top.

Further Expansion

The Minneapolis Brewing Company, and much of the beer business, did fairly well during the 1930s, the time of the Great Depression in the United States, when many other businesses were not doing so well. But even Minneapolis Brewing Company saw its share of problems. There was labor strife in big cities across the country, including Minneapolis, and the home of Grain Belt beer saw its share. The company was under contract with several labor unions, and there were periodic strikes and disputes that often lead to violence in the 1930s. Massive fist fights broke out at an entrance to the plant on at least one occasion when members of one union dared cross the picket lines of another. Numerous arrests and injuries were reported.

Meanwhile, in 1938, Grain Belt's new marketing campaign was "Guaranteed Satisfying," where the company offered a full refund if the beer drinker did not find it the most satisfying beer he ever tasted. And in the spring of 1939, the Minneapolis Brewing Company announced further renovation and expansion of its brewing facilities. As brewery vice president and general manager Charles E. Kiewel wrote in the company magazine The Friendly Faucet in April 1939:

TO ALL FRIENDS OF FRIENDLY GRAIN BELT:

One of the biggest expansion programs in the history of brewing in the Northwest is now nearing completion at the Minneapolis Brewing Company. Hundreds of thousands of dollars have been spent to bring all departments of our huge plant into perfect coordination. A mammoth new stock house has been built capable of increasing our aging facilities by almost 33 1/3 percent. A tremendously big, brand new up-to-the minute bottling unit with automatic pasteurizer has been installed. This machine, our fifth, will turn out beer at the rate of 200 bottles per minute. The brewing

Charles E. Kiewel

facilities of our plant have been expanded and improved so that today no brewery in the country can boast a more beautiful and practical brew house than we have. The engine room and boiler room have had their efficiency doubled. In short, everything humanly possible has been done to assure each one of our distributors and their thousands of retail accounts that we are in a position to meet the constantly increasing demand for our products.

The company did find itself in a bit of controversy in the late 1930s when it distributed an advertising poster of a "Girl in a Barley Field." Featuring a painting of a smiling (fully clothed but well-endowed) young woman lying in a barley field and biting on a stem of barley, with a Grain Belt diamond in the upper-right corner, the poster was considered too suggestive by some. Complaints came in, and the poster was soon withdrawn. Years later, the poster was reproduced by the company as a nostalgia piece.

With the expansion and streamlining of the Minneapolis Brewing Company facilities, the company entered the 1940s with aggressive new advertising and promotional campaigns. Distributor organizations were built throughout Minnesota and the upper Midwest. A new symbol for Grain Belt beer, an outline of a bottle cap behind the familiar red diamond logo that reflected an emphasis on packaged beer, was introduced in 1939 and soon appeared on labels, in advertising and large electric signs, including a massive one erected atop the Marigold Ballroom in Minneapolis in 1940.

When the Marigold Ballroom sign was replaced with another massive electric sign for competing beer Schmidt City Club a few years later, it was reassembled on Nicollet Island near the Hennepin Avenue bridge on the outskirts of downtown Minneapolis, where it would remain an iconic historical landmark decades after the original brewery folded.

The "friendly" theme continued in Grain Belt marketing, with 24-bottle cases promoted as "a case of friendship." Grain Belt also sponsored a radio variety show, "The Friendly Tavern," on powerhouse Minneapolis station WCCO, hosted by Clellen Card.

A somewhat inaccurate depiction of the Grain Belt brewery, with the surrounding buildings in the wrong places, appeared on this late 1930s ink blotter. (Mike Mullally collection)

Friendly Service. The Grain Belt Delivery Force, 1939.

The newly remodeled Grain Belt brewhouse, 1939.

YOU DON'T HAVE TO BE A STRONG MAN!

Big men... little men... anybody can handle a full carton of Grain Belt's new Stein bottles. Thirty per cent shorter, a half pound lighter, Steins still hold the same amount of delicious Grain Belt Beer, but a twenty-four Stein carton is only half the size, seventeen pounds lighter than old unwieldy cases. For the beer with sparkle and tang, for the bottle of convenience and smartness, ask for Grain Belt Beer in STEINS.

EVERY CASE OF GRAIN BELT IS GUARANTEED THE MOST SATISFYING BEER YOU'VE EVER TASTED... OR YOUR MONEY REFUNDED!!!!

MINNEAPOLIS BREWING COMPANY
Minneapolis, Minnesota

Ads and illustrations from the late 1930s.

Served by friendly people at home and in public places...

ASK FOR GRAIN BELT

BEER BOTTLE, MODEL 1936

Charles Kiewel exhibits one of the new "Stein" bottles off the line in April 1936.

The Friendly Faucet was the Minneapolis Brewing Company magazine in the 1930s and early '40s.

1930s era Grain Belt packaging.

Summer 1937 reminder to Grain Belt salesmen.

The Big Brewery Heist

On June 6, 1941, a little after eleven o'clock in the morning, five armed men, later identified as Arthur Lein, Edward Balje, Herman Hymarski, John Hendrixson and James Evans, all of whom were linked to Chicago gangsters, pulled up in a large car to the Minneapolis Brewing Company office building, directly across the street from the brewery on Marshall Street NE. According to various newspaper accounts, the driver stayed at the wheel while the four others entered the building through two entrances, with one standing guard at the front door, carrying sawed-off shotguns and revolvers, and announced, "This is a stick-up!"

The Grain Belt office building in 2018.

With about fifty working in the building at the time, most thought it was a joke, until they saw the guns. Employees and others in the building were ordered to put their hands up as they were herded into the lobby and told to line up against a wall. Two women workers who were gathering files from the basement came up just as the commotion was starting, and were told by one of the bandits to "fall in" and "put your arms up fast" as he waved his gun. They complied. A company truck driver who had entered the office to pick up his paycheck felt the muzzle of a sawed-off shotgun at his back and was told to keep his hands away from his pockets and stand against the wall. The bandits moved quickly in what a newspaper account described as "quiet, confident, professional manner."

The robbery was well planned, and the men seemed to know the place as they went around to each office and common area of the building, demanding money and herding everyone into the front lobby. Almost $50,000 was netted from a cashier's cage. The office kept large amounts of cash on hand to provide check cashing services to employees and customers. One employee, James Christianson, was wounded when one of the bandits fired a shot into the floor as a warning for him to hurry up. The bullet ricocheted and hit Christianson in the shoulder. He was later taken to St. Mary's Hospital in Minneapolis, where he was listed in critical condition, but ultimately recovered.

While this was happening, one of the other bandits went upstairs, where the switchboard and executive offices were. He yanked the headset from operator Min Gillis, and ripped out the wires from the switchboard. Down the hall, the offices of company officials Charles Kiewel, Jacob Kunz and Frank Kiewel were raided.

Frank Kiewel, who was Grain Belt's advertising manager, was on the phone with Hibbing radio station WMFG when one of the bandits announced, "This is a stick-up!" The words were clearly heard over the phone, and the Hibbing radio station had the news on the air seconds later. A man in Kiewel's office who was there to discuss advertising was also ordered to line up with the others.

Old Jacob Kunz, Minneapolis Brewing's Chairman of the Board who had been with the company since 1902 was told, "Come on, snap into it, we're in a hurry."

"Now look here," protested Kunz, "I don't do things in a hurry. You're getting your money. You have nothing to complain of." The robbers netted $150 from his wallet, but didn't get another $50 he had on him.

Jacob Kunz

Louis Findorff

The robbers didn't bother checking the basement where brewery official Louis Findorff was tapping a keg with his brother Rudolph, celebrating his 76th birthday. He heard the commotion upstairs, including the gunshot that was fired, and he and his brother did indeed have about $100 between them. But instead of panicking, he drew himself another noggin of beer.

"If they weren't going to come down and get it, I wasn't going to rush upstairs and hand it over," he told the Minneapolis Times with a chuckle.

Before departing with thousands of stolen dollars in their possession, the leader of the group of bandits shouted at the workers and others huddled in the lobby, "Not a move out of you until we're gone! We've got you covered with machine guns outside, and we're not fooling!"

After the robbers sped away, insurance covered the loss, and the company instituted a policy of not keeping that much cash on site. Minneapolis police and the FBI spent five years investigating. The bandits were traced to Chicago area gangsters in April 1946. The individuals identified had been linked to a number of crimes in Illinois and Minnesota.

World War II

In the early 1940s, Grain Belt packaging further changed. A new label design with a gold background and featuring the red diamond and a bottle cap was introduced. The non-returnable

1940s Grain Belt packaging. The green bottle is from World War II. The two small bottles were novelties that were never actually filled with beer.

stubby bottle, heavily promoted in the '30s, was modified to a lighter weight and less expensive to manufacture glass container, with the words NO DEPOSIT-NO RETURN and NOT TO BE REFILLED embossed in the bottles, to inform consumers who were still inclined to return them to the store. While these improvements were in the works, the United States entered into the Second World War.

The entrance of the United States into World War II brought new challenges to the brewing industry. Canned beer, like Lucky Strike Green, went to war in the 1940s. Tin was rationed, forcing brewers once again to concentrate on marketing in bottles. From 1944 until the end of World War II, federal dictum required that canned beer be produced only for those serving in the Armed Forces. Minneapolis Brewing Company, along with many other brewers, packaged Grain Belt in olive drab cone-top cans, strictly for military use.

For a time, there was even a shortage of brown glass. Many brewers at the time were reluctant to switch back to clear glass because it made it easier for light penetration to ruin the beer and also because of public perception that only cheap beer came in clear bottles. So, for a time, Grain Belt came in green returnable bottles, with a label that said, "This Is Your Regular GRAIN BELT BEER in a TEMPORARY Bottle Due To Bottle Shortage."

Brewers were also required throughout the war to set aside fifteen percent of beer production for exclusive military use. Malt and hops were periodically rationed, making things further difficult for the industry. And, as most breweries employed entirely men for brewing operations, there were shortages of workers as many of these men were called for military service.

At home, keeping the morale up during what often seemed like dark times was a challenge that both the United States Government and private marketers took on. Grain Belt's "friendly" theme fit in with this, promoting the beer as solace and creature comfort that could be enjoyed with friends and could take the edge off of one's troubles and worries, at least for a while. The company gave away a 20-page booklet, "101 Friendly Toasts," published in 1943, with humorous toasts that could be raised with glasses of Grain Belt, including some doses of patriotism, and a few humorous cartoon illustrations.

The war dragged on for a couple more years, but by war's end in 1945, there was a new optimism in the United States, and Minneapolis Brewing Company, along with the rest of the industry, came back in full force. Service men came home from Europe and the Pacific, thirsty for their hometown brews as they moved back into civilian life. While some of them went to the bars to celebrate upon their return, it wasn't something they wanted to do night after night. Sales of on tap beer continued to drop as home consumption saw further increases and more households were purchasing refrigerators. Grain Belt advertising would be geared toward the at-home, family consumer, emphasizing the "friendly" theme.

Grain Belt newspaper ads featuring the bottle cap logo.

It's Been a Long Time a-Brewing

Grain Belt packaging was redesigned again at the turn of the decade into the 1950s. Bavarian-style lettering replaced the block capital letters on the red diamond, and a unique die-cut label began to appear. Meanwhile, a new formula beer, dubbed Grain Belt Premium, was developed in 1947, and was test marketed with positive results. Minnehaha Ale (a product with little relation to the Prohibition-era Minnehaha Pale) was later introduced, in green bottles.

Grain Belt's future in the post-war era was in the hands of Frank Kiewel, nephew of Minneapolis Brewing Company president and chairman of the board Charles E. Kiewel. Starting with the company right after Repeal, he was advertising manager from 1936-1949, director of sales and advertising from 1949-1951, and on September 18, 1951, he was named president of Minneapolis Brewing Company.

As ad manager and director, Frank Kiewel's singular focus was putting and keeping Grain Belt before the public eye, and Minneapolis Brewing Company's board of directors voted to entrust the company's future to him.

Grain Belt Premium sponsored nightly broadcasts of the Bohemian Band on WNAX Radio in Yankton, SD.

The younger Kiewel had his work cut out for him. Trouble was brewing in the brewing industry as America entered the 1950s. Beer consumption began to decline after an immediate post-war peak. Grain Belt sales slipped to under 500,000 barrels. The cumulative effect of Prohibition and the war, in addition to declining sales, took its toll on the entire industry. Even Anheuser-Busch, then and now the nation's largest brewer, operated on a three-day work week through most of 1954. Breweries all over the country were folding, including Minnesota's first, the Yoerg Brewing Company of St. Paul, which brewed its final batch of beer in 1952 after 104 years.

Minneapolis Brewing and its up-the-street neighbor Gluek would suffer tremendously in July 1955 when a strike shut down the two breweries for two weeks. July was the typical peak month for beer consumption so the strike couldn't have happened at a worse time.

Frank Kiewel

By the time the workers were back on the job toward the end of the month, Minneapolis Brewing suffered a net loss of $64,000 for the first seven months of 1955. Similar losses were reported at Gluek. Detroit-based Pfeiffer Brewing Company looked into acquiring Minneapolis Brewing, but they ultimately took over St. Paul-based Jacob Schmidt in 1956.

Adding to the company's woes was a proxy fight threatened by a minority group of shareholders for control of the company. It was averted and a similar threat the next year didn't materialize. Grain Belt was bruised a little, but it wasn't down.

Early 1950s Grain Belt bottles and cone-top cans.

"The Heritage of America's Grain Belt," published in 1952.

America's Party Beer-- Advertised in LIFE.

Advertising Blitz

With the former head of advertising now running the company, Minneapolis Brewing Company was off and running in the 1950s with the biggest advertising blitz for Grain Belt beer in the company's history. One of the first ad campaigns of the decade was called "America's Grain Belt," celebrating the lore and heritage of the upper Midwest region where finest grains are grown to produce the best beer. The company published a promotional booklet called "The Heritage of America's Grain Belt," with color drawings and profiles of the states of Minnesota, North Dakota, South Dakota, Iowa and Wisconsin, and the "friendly land." The sixteen-page, 8"x10.5" booklet looked a bit like something that could have been handed out to grade school classes, and perhaps it was, in spite of the beer advertising.

In 1953, Grain Belt was promoted as "America's Party Beer." That theme appeared in a half page, one color advertisement in the May 18, 1953 issue of Life, then the nation's most popular magazine. A smaller ad appeared in subsequent issues. During this campaign, the Life magazine logo even appeared on Grain Belt bottle labels and other Grain Belt advertising.

The new ad campaigns were still missing the mark and Grain Belt's troubles continued with poor sales, changing consumer habits and internal labor issues. The company enlisted Minneapolis-based advertising agency Knox Reeves to re-image Grain Belt and get it back on top.

With extensive research on the market and competitive beer advertising, they came up with a new theme: Diamond Clear—Smoother Beer, putting emphasis on the diamond-shaped logo that had been associated with Grain Belt since the 1890s. The labeling was changed in 1954 to a design featuring red and gold diamonds. Golden Grain Belt beer in brown bottles continued to be the main product, while marketing of smoother Premium Grain Belt in clear (or flint) bottles was expanded. To explain to prospective consumers why Grain Belt is "Diamond Clear," Brewmaster Frank

Mathes came up with the perfect slogan: Because "it's been a long time a-brewing."

While newspapers had been a main advertising outlet for Grain Belt in the past, the emphasis henceforth would be on billboards, radio and the new medium of television. There were three television stations on the air in the Twin Cities by 1953, with a fourth going on in early 1955, plus many more scattered around the state and further out in Grain Belt's upper Midwest marketing area.

The first Grain Belt television commercials hit the airwaves in 1954 featuring animated glasses of beer with cartoon faces dancing to a jingle that sang, "It's light, it's Golden Grain Belt." The next year another campaign of animated spots was introduced, featuring humorous spoofs of historic figures such as Cleopatra, Napoleon, Mata Hari and Christopher Columbus, with voices done by Mel Blanc of Bugs Bunny fame, and hitting the theme, "Grain Belt Beer is Diamond Clear!"

"It's light. It's Golden Grain Belt!" Dancing glasses from the first Grain Belt TV commercial.

The strategy by Knox Reeves in focusing on electronic and outdoor media for Grain Belt advertising was explained in the June 1955 issue of the Grain Belt Diamond, the new official company magazine. "Television because you retain 10 percent of what you hear, 50 percent of what you see and 75 percent of what you see and hear; and radio because it reaches into areas where television is not reaching…in every corner of the house, the kitchen, car, bedroom, basement, etc. Outdoor advertising was used because it hits people when they're on the way to the store or to the tavern with money to spend. Everyone goes out of doors."

The Modernization of Grain Belt

In the summer of 1955, Minneapolis Brewing Company discontinued the use of cap-sealed "cone-top" cans for Grain Belt beer after 20 years, and switched to flat-top cans that required a punch-type opener (or "church key" as they were popularly called) to open the cans. The cans were cheaper than the cone tops and were more practical, especially for storage. By the end of the 1950s, the cap-sealed cone top cans were being used almost entirely for automotive additives, as the top made the perfect

Ground Rules for Flat Top Cans — One, Two, Three Sip

1 FOR DRINKING — J. Raymond Fox, new Grain Belt vice president in charge of sales, demonstrates the correct way to open the new flat top cans FOR DRINKING. By punching two holes in the can, the beer will flow freely, and less carbon dioxide, which causes foam clogging the opening, will escape.

2 FOR POURING—Punching only one hole in the flat top can, Fox shows the way to open the new cans FOR POURING Grain Belt into a glass. One hole releases the excess carbon dioxide gas, causing more foam and a bigger head on the beer in the glass.

3 HERE'S TO YOU—Ready to sip, Fox proposes a Grain Belt toast in the Minneapolis Brewing Company Friendship Room with the new flat top can. This is one of the few times Fox has been motionless since his appointment as vice president of the brewery.

Brewery official J. Raymond Fox demonstrates the proper way to open Grain Belt's new flat top can, from the Grain Belt Diamond, August 1955.

funnel.

Minneapolis Brewing Company was on the rebound. In October 1955, the newly re-designed Grain Belt Premium bottle label won the Brewers Association of America Grand Championship Award for best label in the U.S., from a field of 400 entries from around the country, at the organization's conclave in Chicago. The company went on to win several other awards at the conclave, ranging from bottle caps to matchbook covers to trays and other merchandise.

A new program of modernization at the brewery began with new, more efficient equipment replacing old equipment in the bottle house, and expansion of the warehouse. A new malt mill, weighing six and a half tons, was shipped in from Braunschweig, Germany and installed on the third floor of the brew house. Several windows and part of an outside wall had to be taken out in order to get the mill into the

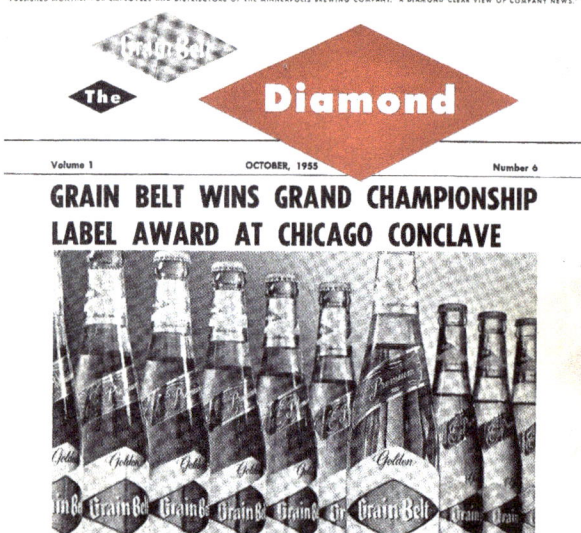

Award-winning label for Grain Belt Premium, touted on the cover of the October 1955 Grain Belt Diamond company newsletter.

building, using hoisting equipment.

In spite of a shaky start to the year, sales were increasing. A record 66,000 cases were loaded into distributors' trucks in one day on July 11, 1955. Grain Belt's Moose Lake distributor Sid Lee treated warehouse employees, who had worked well into the night, to a Dutch lunch, according to an article in the August 1955 Grain Belt Diamond. In addition to that, Grain Belt products received international recognition when the Museo Universal De Bedidas, in Madrid, Spain, the world's largest museum of liquors, wines and beers, requested bottles of Grain Belt Premium and Minnehaha Ale for the museum's American beer exhibit.

At the beginning of 1956, Rome Sexton, Minneapolis Brewing Company secretary, stated, "We have a wonderful sales promotion and advertising program at Grain Belt, and I am looking forward to a bright, sparkling year for the company in 1956."

Expansion and modernization continued. In February 1956, it was announced that Grain Belt Premium, in the clear bottles with the award-winning label, would be available in all retail outlets, after being tested in twenty markets. Meanwhile, Grain Belt's market continued to expand. The company added a distributorship in Chicago, its first there since Prohibition. More new distributors were added in Illinois, Iowa, Wisconsin, Michigan, North Dakota, South Dakota, Montana and Wyoming. There was even a Grain Belt distributor in Anchorage, Alaska, which also distributed the beer 3,000 miles away to a supper club in Fairbanks called the Golden Slipper, which advertised, "Dancing, Mixed Drinks, Beer, Ale, Wine (even Grain Belt, too!)."

The label design continued to evolve. The Bavarian-style lettering in the Grain Belt logo was phased out, with the name appearing in more modern, sans serif font. The red cans were redesigned with a gold diamond-patterned background, making the red Grain Belt logo stand out more.

In the spring of 1956, Minnesota's first Major League ballpark, Metropolitan Stadium, opened up in Bloomington, serving as the new home of the minor league Minneapolis Millers until a Major League team could be brought in. Grain Belt was prominent at the new stadium, sharing advertising space with Gluek, the other Minneapolis beer, on the big electronic scoreboard directly across from home plate. Both brands, naturally, were served there as well. Grain Belt had signage at the old Nicollet Park in south Minneapolis, the Millers' former home.

By the end of 1956, sales of all Minneapolis Brewing Company brands had risen, while Hamm's, Schmidt and Gluek saw declines.

ON WITH THE NEW—Much more to her liking, and the general public's as well, Beverly holds the new six pak carton which eliminates tearing the top of the package and makes it easier to remove the Grain Belt cans.

From the Grain Belt Diamond, September 1955.

six new mdse'ing aids... been long time a-brewing

TIME ON MY HANDS . . . There shouldn't be time or Grain Belt on anyone's hands with proper use of store domination sign.

IVY . . . poisonous for slow sales. The combination hurricane lamp and ivy-surrounded Grain Belt diamond on a tweed background will put the sizzle in the sell of our products.

SUMMERTIME APPEAL . . . This catch is good for the fisherman and the retailer. Part of a series that has been ever-popular, the piece should demonstrate its popularity in extra cases.

BATTER UP . . . for better sales. A seasonal tie-in with trouble light forming catcher's mask provides excellent opportunity for mass displays of six packs in on and off sale establishments. This should be worth ten extra cases.

A LITTLE LIGHT ON THE SUBJECT . . . heat motor lamp in contemporary black wrought iron has revolving bulb inside that gives impression of movement to letters "Grain Belt beer is diamond clear."

Grain Belt Six Pack Comes To Life

KING SIZE DANCING SIX PAK—An invitation to a masquerade party was the inspiration for this unusual costume worn by staff members and wives of Knox Reeves Advertising, Inc., agency for the Minneapolis Brewing Company. A month's work was devoted to constructing the human six pak, which magnifies the newly designed Grain Belt package. Wives of the team added the chapeau idea in the form of bottle crowns, made from crinkled paper plates and painted red and gold, Minneapolis Brewing Company colors.

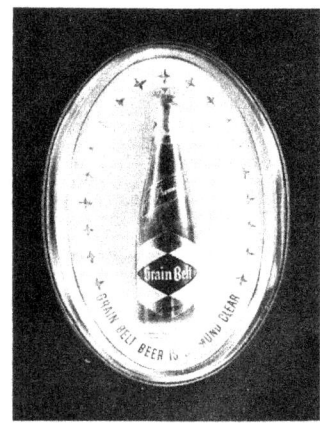

SPOTLIGHT ON PREMIUM . . . This piece sells Grain Belt AND the company. It's good enough to hang over your own fireplace, but it belongs in the retailer's place of business who knows how to use it . . . profitably.

Grain Belt merchandise, from the May 1955 issue of the Grain Belt Diamond. The six-pack costume shown at the lower left was a one-of-a-kind piece.

A few "Friendly Facts" about one of the 360-barrel storage tanks at the Grain Belt brewery.

TIME OUT FOR A TOAST—During the bowling league's first meeting, Minneapolis Brewing Company employees, Gene Roback, Elmer Hansen, John Berg, Dick Woodbury and Joe Stanek proposed a Grain Belt toast to the success of the league during the coming year.

Members of the official Grain Belt bowling league (all Minneapolis Brewing Company employees) raise a toast in the Friendship Room at the brewery during a meeting on August 17, 1955.
(From the Grain Belt Diamond, September 1955.)

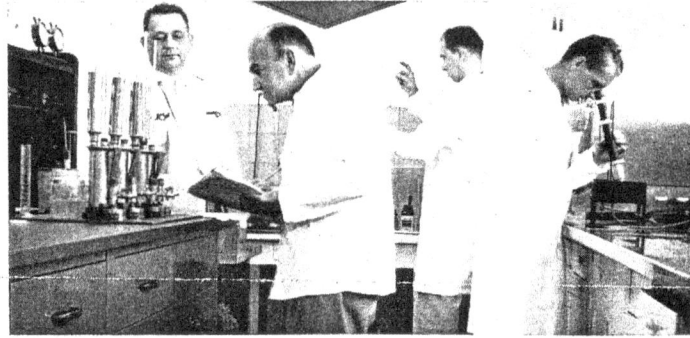

Brewmaster Frank Mathes (left) heads quality control staff at Minneapolis Brewing Co. Other members of staff are Bill Job, assistant chemist; Harland Anderson, chief chemist and Werner Kolb, assistant chemist. Grain Belt and Gluek labs are leaders in quality control measures and are known throughout the brewing industry in the United States for their up-to-date equipment.

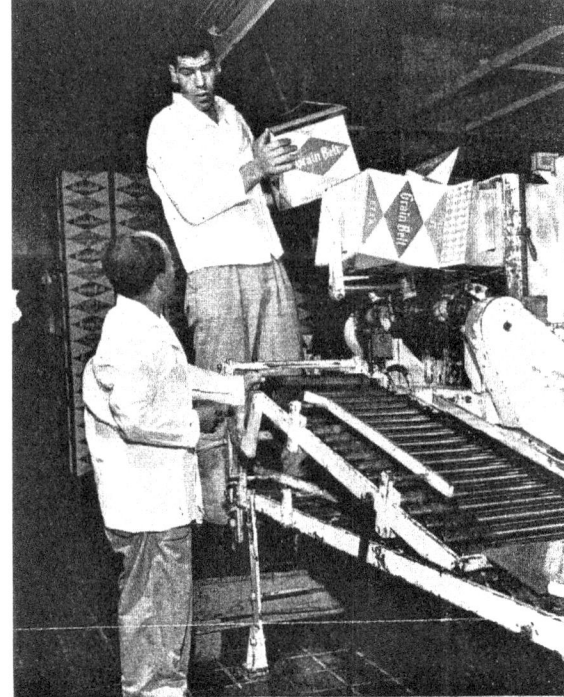

The long and short of the brewing industry are 4' 11" Walter Wrobel and 6' 10" Bill Simon U. of M. cager who works at Minneapolis Brewing Co. during summer months. The two Mut Jeffers are working on a modern case loader at Grain Belt's main plant, 1215 Marshall St.

Frank Kiewel, president, Minneapolis Brewing Co., and Art Gluek, president, Gluek Brewing Co., toast each other with steins of beer. The two companies have always maintained friendly relations.

Friendly relations. Illustrations from an October 1954 article in Greater Minneapolis magazine profiling the Grain Belt and Gluek breweries. Frank Kiewel and Arthur Gluek raise a toast at lower left.

Stanley and Albert

In the early days of television commercials, animation was frequently utilized to advertise countless products. It was an effective marketing device in the new medium that got viewers' attention. Grain Belt used animation in its earliest TV ads, while St. Paul-based rival Hamm's struck a chord with a cartoon bear in their commercials.

With a marketing strategy that focused on billboards and television, it was only fitting that in 1956 Grain Belt and the Knox Reeves agency would come up with a couple of animated cartoon sign painters, called Stanley and Albert, as advertising characters for their television commercials, promoting Grain Belt Premium. Stanley was the bespectacled little guy and Albert was the big lug with a deep voice, singing a jingle that went (something along the lines of) "I'm Stanley, he's Albert, Yes it's Diamond Clear, Been a Long-Long Time a-Brewing... Grain Belt Premium Beer…"

Along with television commercials, Stanley and Albert

The new look of Grain Belt Premium, in gold flat-top cans.

appeared on billboards (naturally), promotional glasses and mugs, print ads, matchbooks (where users were encouraged by the characters to close the cover so they "don't set fire to us"), point-of-purchase store displays, indoor signs and other items. Live actors (usually Grain Belt employees) portrayed Stanley and Albert at events such as the Minneapolis Aquatennial parade in July, and in other parades and events around Minnesota.

Meanwhile, by 1958, Minneapolis Brewing Company continued to expand with increased sales of Grain Belt beer, new equipment in the brew house, keg house and bottling house, where capacity of all eight bottling and canning lines was increased to approximately 2,500 packages per minute, the introduction of two new products and the purchase of the Kiewel Brewing Company in Little Falls, Minnesota.

One of the new products introduced was Wunderbar, a stronger, hopier brew, promoted as "European Style" and made in the old German

"European Style" Wunderbar Pilsner Supreme.

tradition, unlike the vast majority of American beers in the late 1950s and beyond. The Wunderbar cans had a bi-lingual label and the TV commercials were spoken in German with English subtitles, an unusual sales tactic for the time. It was a specialty beer some forty years before specialty beers would come into vogue.

Wunderbar appealed primarily to older beer drinkers, including those who still remembered what beer tasted like before Prohibition. It was served at some of the finer restaurants, including the Black Steer in Milwaukee of all places, the home of several large breweries.

In 1959, Minneapolis Brewing bought the Kiewel Brewing Company of Little Falls, Minnesota. The company namesake, Jacob Kiewel, was the grandfather of Minneapolis Brewing Company president Frank Kiewel. But blood ties aside, all the Kiewel brands were discontinued and the company began making White Label, a discount brand, at the Little Falls plant that spring. (A former Kiewel brand was called White Seal.)

The Little Falls brewery was operated until January 1961, when officials determined that White Label sales had outgrown the plant's 40,000-barrel capacity, a claim called 'dubious' by some. Production of White Label was moved to Minneapolis and the Kiewel plant was closed.

STANLEY AND ALBERT RAISE GRAINBELT SALES WITH HAPPY TV ANTICS

The happy antics of Stanley and Albert, the Minneapolis Brewing Company's sign-painting salesmen, are seen by WTCN-TV viewers several times per week.

They appear in both 20-second and one-minute commercials in a night-time heavy saturation schedule on WTCN-TV.

Brewery representatives report a growth in sales of Grain Belt Premium due to Stanley and Albert's efforts.

The success of the Stanley & Albert campaign was touted in a 1958 WTCN-TV (Channel 11) sales brochure. (Roger Awsumb collection)

Minneapolis Brewing Company grew at a time of industry stagnation. The company spent $4.5 million expanding and renovating its brewery over a six-year period beginning in 1956, including $1.3 million in 1960 to add a new automated fermenting cellar, which was said to be the first in the industry. The cellar held 22 fermenting tanks, each with a 1,500-barrel capacity. Also added was a new 550-barrel brew kettle and automated bottling lines, with made it possible for empty returnable beer bottles to enter the brewery, be removed from the cases, go through the washing process, be refilled, capped, put in new cases and sent out without ever being touched by human hands.

Kid Cann Connections

Minneapolis Brewing Company was accused of having ties to the notorious Minneapolis gangster known as Kid Cann in the early 1960s. At the 1961 trial of members of a liquor syndicate controlled by Kid Cann (born Isadore Blumenfeld in 1900, died in 1981), that was held in Federal Court in St. Paul, it was alleged that Minneapolis Brewing Company gave a 30 cent price advantage per case of Grain Belt beer to stores and taverns controlled by the syndicate.

After the trial, eighteen beer retailers who were not involved with the Kid Cann syndicate sued the brewery for $8 million in Hennepin County District Court. The suit asked that the company be required to refund the retailers thirty cents for each case of Grain Belt sold in Hennepin County from 1955 to 1961. The suit claimed that the alleged deal between the brewery and the syndicate constituted an "illegal bargain" and that it "amounted to price discrimination in favor of a few retailers, contrary to state law.

Hennepin County district judge Irving Brand dismissed the complaint in December 1961, on the grounds that it failed to offer a basis for relief. An amended complaint was filed the following month,

Stanley & Albert greeted visitors to the Grain Belt brewery in 1958.

only to be dismissed again by Judge Brand, who said that the new complaint failed to include allegations of damages to cure the deficiencies of the original complaint.

Moving into the Big League '60s

The strength of Grain Belt, Hamm's, Schmidt and to a smaller extent Gluek's made it difficult for the huge national brands such as Budweiser and Miller to make a significant dent in Minnesota beer sales. The four big regionals controlled over 75 percent of the Minnesota beer market. Minneapolis Brewing Company alone contributed about seventeen percent of the state's beer production, helping make Minnesota the ninth largest beer producer in the United States. Grain Belt was at or near the top of sales in Minnesota and the Dakotas, and it was sold as far west as Arizona, Wyoming, Colorado and even Alaska.

In 1961, five years after Metropolitan Stadium opened in Bloomington, MN for minor league baseball, Minnesota went big league when the Minnesota Twins (the former Washington Senators) moved into the Met, as well as the National Football League's expansion Minnesota Vikings later that year. Grain Belt continued to have a prominent presence at the stadium with a billboard above the newly re-built scoreboard as well as on the "welcome sign" in the stadium's main parking lot, and it was one of four local beers (Grain Belt and Gluek's from Minneapolis, Hamm's and Schmidt from St. Paul) available at the stadium. When the Vikings arrived in the fall, Grain Belt sponsored a weekly television show featuring coach Norm Van Brocklin on WCCO-TV Channel 4.

The most exciting times yet for Grain Belt, however, were just around the corner.

Major League Baseball at Metropolitan Stadium was the theme for Grain Belt's float in the Hopkins, MN Raspberry Days parade.

DIAMOND CLEAR PUNCH

Get an oversize bowl and mix the following ingredients in the order given. Stir well, and add as much ice as possible. Serve when chilled.

Grapefruit Juice, 2 quarts
Weak black tea, 1 quart
Lemon Juice, 1 cup
Light Puerto Rican Rum, 1 quart
Strong Grain Belt Premium Beer, 8 twelve-ounce bottles
Sugar to taste, about a cup. Remember, always put the beer in just ahead of the sugar.

From the Grain Belt Diamond, October 1962

A couple of interesting labels from the late 1950s to early 1960s. Grain Belt Premium quart, and Sportsman's Grain Belt Beer, featuring scenes of hunting, fishing, golf and outdoor cooking.

Get ready for the weekend with a double supply of Premium.

Ask for GRAIN BELT PREMIUM at the State Fair and at your County Fair.

Stanley & Albert promoted Grain Belt Premium in the local program pages of the August 29, 1960 issue of TV Guide. The beach scene might raise politically correct eyebrows today...

The Grain Belt "Talking Scoreboard" was a radio with a lighted scoreboard that could be used by bars during broadcasts of baseball and football games. Score was kept by the bartender with a grease marker on the plastic display. Baseball and football inserts were available.

On your holiday trip, take along a little *extra* Grain Belt Premium

Take your cue from Stanley and Albert —be sure to get a little *extra* Premium for the long holiday weekend. Whether your plans are as big as all outdoors, or the small, take-it-easy-at-home kind, you'll find that the wonderful, sparkling refreshment of Premium fits them perfectly. Grain Belt Premium... diamond clear, smoother beer!

Stanley and Albert ride the rails for Grain Belt Premium in this 1960 ad.

The best kitchens serve Good Food and Grain Belt Premium, natually.

Welcome To Grain Belt Park

Postcard image of Grain Belt Park on Broadway Avenue and Marshall Street, in front of the Minneapolis Brewing Company brewhouse with the office building at right.

In early 1963, a fenced off area in front of the Grain Belt brewery on the busy corner of Broadway Avenue and Marshall Street NE, with some shabby buildings and piles of junk, underwent a major change. The area was landscaped with gardens, trees were planted, and the exterior of the buildings was remodeled to look like a Bavarian wayside inn, transforming the unsightly corner into a scenic new Grain Belt Park, dedicated on June 24, 1963.

The park dedication was attended by brewery officials, Grain Belt distributors, civic leaders and other VIPs. At the center of the park, a giant Grain Belt bottle cap topped a pile of boulders. An "uncapping ceremony" was held, and with the removal of the cap, water came gushing out from the boulders, shooting up eighteen feet high and flowing back down into the area below. Dedicated as the Diamond Wells Fountain, the water, it was said, came from a well some 1,074 feet underground. Bavarian dancers and music were also part of the ceremonies. A tap room and tour center called the "Gasthaus" (German for "Guest House") was opened as part of the "Bavarian Inn," all of which made Grain Belt Park an oasis and tourist attraction in the middle of a busy industrial area of Minneapolis. A depiction of the fountain soon appeared in Grain Belt advertising and labels as a secondary trade mark, with the slogan, "From Perfect Brewing Water."

Grain Belt Park was an instant hit with the public, attracting tourists and sight seers to the brewery, garnering positive publicity and accolades from the community and advocates for urban beautification. At the end of the 1963 summer season, over 1,500 people had visited Grain Belt Park. The park closed to the public in the fall, but the Diamond Wells Fountain continued to flow

24 hours a day, through the winter and into the next season.

Meanwhile the park was expanded in time for the 1964 season, continuing the Bavarian motif from Marshall Street all the way over to Ramsey Street. Adding to the attraction, tame deer were brought to the park. The visitors loved the deer, but unfortunately security had to be increased after an October 1964 incident when two men broke into the wooden pen where the deer were kept, killing one and injuring another. The men were apprehended and sentenced to prison, according to an article in the July 1965 Grain Belt Diamond.

In 1965, the park atmosphere was expanded yet again with the opening of Grain Belt Concert Park, directly across Broadway Avenue from Grain Belt Park, offering free to the public Sunday evening open air band concerts, performed by Elmo Lunkley's 35-piece Symphonic Band.

The Diamond Wells Fountain at dusk in the summertime.

According to the July 1965 Grain Belt Diamond, "A variety of music—marches, Dixieland jazz, waltzes, soloists and Broadway musical comedy tunes—is offered each Sunday…Each concert opens with the playing of 'America' and 'Give a Little Whistle,' Grain Belt's theme song (used in TV and radio jingles at the time), and concludes with 'The Star Spangled Banner.'"

Thousands attended these Sunday events, including many families with children, sitting in the grass and enjoying live music. Refreshment trucks were there, but no beer was served.

Billy Martin and Grain Belt

The Minneapolis Brewing Company had at least one famous employee in the 1960s. Billy Martin, third base coach and later manager of the Minnesota Twins, joined Grain Belt as a special sales representative and public relations man in 1962, the year he came to Minnesota. In that capacity, he helped whip up the Grain Belt sales team, made speeches and gave public appearances on behalf of the company during baseball's off-season.

When Martin was fired by Twins owner Calvin Griffith in 1969, he remained in Minnesota and with Grain Belt, which co-sponsored a baseball themed radio show he hosted on local station

KDWB, until 1971 when he left to join the Detroit Tigers. Martin later came to be known for his stints with the Oakland A's and New York Yankees and for his tumultuous relationship with Yankees owner George Steinbrenner. He died in a single-vehicle car crash in New York on December 25, 1989, at age 61.

New packaging and ad campaigns

In the mid-1960s, Grain Belt began to appear on store shelves in new "easy opening" non-returnable packaging. Quart bottles were filled and topped with resealable twist-off caps, enabling the beer drinker to pour a glass then replace the cap and put the bottle back in the refrigerator, where the beer would remain palatable for at least a day or two.

Around 1965, tab tops began to appear on Grain Belt cans, where one could pull an attached tab on the aluminum top (the cans themselves were still made of tin-plated steel) and open the can without a separate opener. The early versions, however, could be difficult to grip and pull open, so improvements were made, such as replacing the tab with a ring that was easier to grip. Grain Belt also tested a pull tab cap on non-returnable bottles, which proved to be even more difficult to open. Grain Belt introduced tall 16-ounce cans around this time as

THAT'S OUR BEER say three principals involved in planning the Grain Belt-WDGY sports champion dinner. From left, Charles Loufek, WDGY account executive; Billy Martin, main speaker, and Luke Laskow, Grain Belt advertising manager.

Billy Martin (center) at the Grain Belt-WDGY Sports Championship Dinner. From the Grain Belt Diamond, December 1965.

well.

    Meanwhile, Stanley and Albert were phased out of Grain Belt advertising as the company embarked on campaigns that emphasized "Perfect Brewing Water." Around fifty percent of the company's advertising budget went into outdoor signs, and Grain Belt billboards, showing a photo of the product in various settings with some sort of humorous line along the bottom, won praise and awards for their clever simplicity.

    Grain Belt billboards seemed to be everywhere in the Twin Cities and throughout Minnesota. Some of the award-winning and memorable ones in the late '60s included "Take our best with the wurst" (showing a mug of Grain Belt with liverwurst), "Swallow our pride" (someone drinking from a bottle of Grain Belt Premium), "Diamonds are a grill's best friend" (Grain Belt diamonds with foods on a grill), "Super suds" (a foaming mug of Grain Belt), "One pitcher is worth 1,000 words" (a glass pitcher full of Grain Belt), "Everyone's putting us down" (someone setting down a just-emptied mug of Grain Belt on a bar), "Create a frank 'n stein" (a frankfurter on a bun with a stein of Grain Belt) and many others.

New, ostensibly "easy-opening" tab devices began appearing on Grain Belt bottles and cans in the mid 1960s.

Been a long time a-BRUIN. Grain Belt sponsored broadcasts of Minneapolis Bruins minor league hockey on WLOL Radio and WTCN-TV Channel 11. The team only lasted for two seasons, from 1963-65. (Dave Wendl collection)

Grain Belt Breweries, Inc.

As the 1960s rolled on, Grain Belt continued to do extremely well as a regional brewer in a time when the industry was losing steam in some places and a lot of regional brewers, such as the Gluek Brewing Company just a few blocks north on Marshall Street NE, were going out of business. Grain Belt sales had reached 25th in the nation in 1966, according to company president and general manager Frank Kiewel at a shareholder's meeting.

The company was doing well but in order to continue to thrive in the highly competitive industry, it had to expand. The company had built several additions to its property over the years and there wasn't much room for further expansion on the site. Hamm's of St. Paul continued to be the top local brewer, in part by acquiring breweries in Los Angeles, San Francisco, Baltimore and Houston (the latter two of which proved unsuccessful for that company).

In May 1967, Minneapolis Brewing Company announced it would be taking over management of the 91-year-old Storz Brewing Company of Omaha, Nebraska effective June 1 in a lease agreement which included an option to buy, and with that, the company officially changed its name to Grain Belt Breweries, Inc. Frank Kiewel explained the new company name would "provide stronger product identification and underscore the firm's widening area of marketing operations"

as well as "shed the image of a long-ago business." The company had been commonly referred to as Grain Belt rather than Minneapolis Brewing Company for years anyway.

The Storz brewery had a rated capacity of 750,000 barrels and the company's products were primarily marketed in Nebraska, Iowa, South Dakota and Kansas with limited distribution in surrounding states, according to the June 1967 issue of the Grain Belt Diamond. The Storz portfolio put Grain Belt into the ranks of the top 20 brewers nationally.

With the Omaha brewery operating as Storz Division, Grain Belt Breweries, Inc., Grain Belt continued to produce Storz Premium and Storz Triumph beers at both facilities. Grain Belt labels now listed two cities and radio commercials ended with the tagline, "Grain Belt Beer. Minneapolis, Omaha and other thirsty places."

The move, at least in the beginning, proved to be quite successful for Grain Belt. Frank Kiewel reported that sales and earnings for the third quarter of 1969 at both the Minneapolis and Omaha breweries were well ahead of the same period in 1968, and on August 26, 1969 it was announced that Grain Belt would exercise its option to buy the Storz Brewing Company effective January 1, 1970, with Kiewel reiterating that Grain Belt was "in Omaha to stay."

BREWED & BOTTLED BY JOHN HAUENSTEIN CO., NEW ULM, MINN.

Looking to further expand the company portfolio, Grain Belt made an unsuccessful bid to acquire the Blatz label from the Pabst Brewing Company of Milwaukee in 1969 (it ultimately went to the G. Heileman Brewing Company of La Crosse, Wisconsin). Grain Belt did, however, acquire the Hauenstein brand and formula from the John Hauenstein Company of New Ulm, Minnesota in February 1970, after that brewery closed down in late 1969 after 105 years in business. The small town brewer was no longer able to compete with the large regionals such as Grain Belt or the big national brewers. Hauenstein president Roger Schmid was retained by Grain Belt as a consultant for the brand.

Under Grain Belt, the labels continued to read "Hauenstein New Ulm Beer," even though it was now brewed in Minneapolis. Grain Belt began putting Hauenstein beer in cans for the first time since about 1960, when the old New Ulm brewery discontinued cone-top cans. The new Hauenstein cans had pull tab tops. The beer was sold only in bottles and cans, and was not offered on draft.

Meanwhile, Grain Belt continued to make improvements at its Minneapolis facility, both inside and out. In 1967, a Strainmaster automated system and control panel, standing 14 feet

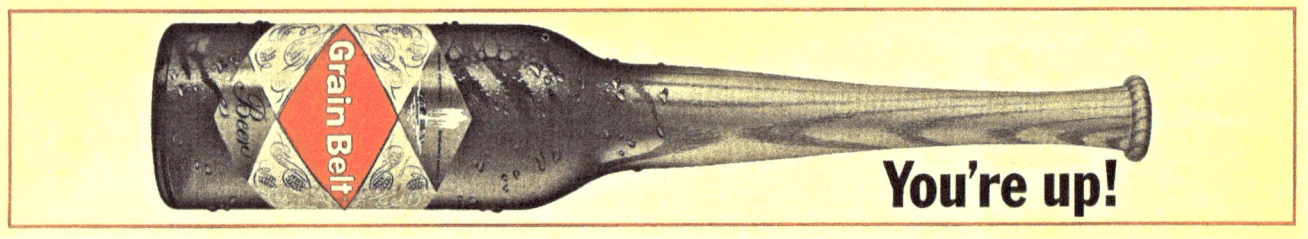

Grain Belt banners and billboards appeared on Minnesota Twins scorecards and above the big scoreboard at Metropolitan Stadium. These examples are from 1967 and 1970.

high by 10 feet wide and weighing 20 tons, was installed on the fourth floor of the Grain Belt brewhouse, increasing brewing capacity at the Minneapolis plant by 33%.

Improvements were made to the outside park as well, as it continued to be a popular attraction in the city and a place for local events. Two cast iron storks, named Hansel and Gretel, kept vigil over Grain Belt Park from a nest up above. "No matter how exciting, how enjoyable the events below may be, these birds never ruffle a feather," reported the Grain Belt Diamond.

In addition to that, in 1969 the mural on the side of the Grain Belt brewhouse facing the park was repainted, replacing what for years had served as a billboard featuring product labels and slogans, with a plain red diamond corporate logo over blue and white painted brick with the words "Grain Belt Breweries, Inc." above the diamond, to blend in more with the scenery. The move was made in response to concerns from community activists and advocates for urban beautification. The new mural drew praise, with the Women's Division of the Minneapolis Chamber of Commerce inviting Frank Kiewel to speak to them about the company's efforts, and Minneapolis Star columnist Barbara Flanagan (quoted in the Grain Belt Diamond) commenting that it "looks great now" and "isn't it nice to know that's one historic site that won't come down for a parking lot?"

With the increasing popularity of throwaway beer containers, litter was increasingly becoming an issue. Some state legislatures were introducing bills to ban the use of all non-returnable beer and soft drink containers, something the industry did not want to see happen. Grain Belt's paper cartons for non-returnable packaging carried the message, "Help keep our countryside beautiful, dispose of empty cartons and bottles or cans in proper containers." The company worked with its distributors to organize cleanup campaigns and distribute litter bags for cars and trucks.

As the Grain Belt Diamond said in its September 1968 issue, "For years there was a fallacy among many distributors and personnel that 6-pak (sic) cartons, bottles and cans strewn along the highway were good advertising. How Erroneous! ...This junk along the highway will do no more than call adverse attention to the brewing industries. It is poor advertising. Do your part in the litter campaign – Keep America Beautiful."

The 1960s were the best decade ever for Grain Belt, with the company seeing its greatest growth and most significant changes. Beer production at Grain Belt had reached one million barrels for the first time in 1967, achieving that goal a year earlier than had been expected. In April 1970, Grain Belt reported profits were up by $2,000 in the first quarter, with

The new look of Grain Belt Park.

sales up nine percent. A new bottling warehouse and can handling plant were being built, and company president Frank Kiewel told stockholders that the company was engaged in the acquisition of other companies "both in and out of the brewing industry" without further elaboration.

Grain Belt entered the '70s in a strong position, ranking as the 18th largest brewer in the country. But big changes in the industry were to come.

The New Brew for the New Breed

In the summer of 1970, Grain Belt introduced an all-new product with an aggressive advertising campaign, GBX Malt Liquor, in an embossed silver can with blue racing stripes. Malt liquors were becoming a popular thing at the time, with Schlitz Malt Liquor ("the Bull") leading the way, although the very first malt liquor was actually Gluek Stite, made by the old Gluek Brewing Company up the street from Grain Belt in Minneapolis going back some 20 years earlier.

Grain Belt had done extensive market research on malt liquors going back to 1967, finding they were especially popular with college students, urban blacks, "swingers," the affluent and young people in general, all potential growth demographics for Grain Belt. Grain Belt's

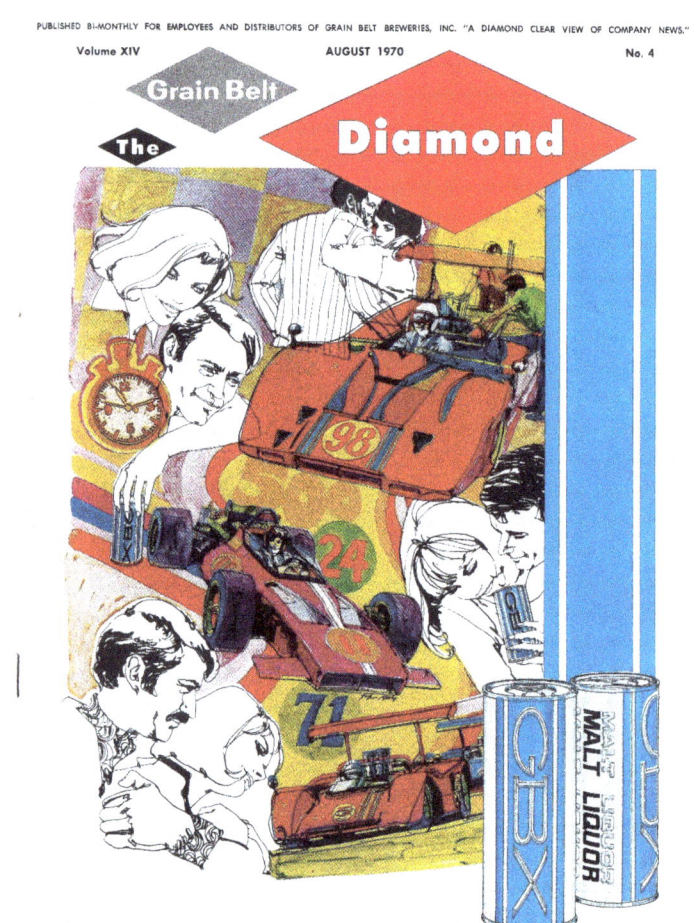

Brewmaster Frank Mathes created the formula, with the mission of finding something "with authority, but smooth in taste," "without aftertaste" and "low enough in carbonation, but strong enough to produce head and cling," according to the August 1970 Grain Belt Diamond.

As for the name GBX, the Diamond reported, "Grain Belt drinkers would recognize the name's association with the brewery. And, in new territory, GBX had the impact to pave its own way. There was the magic of the unknown 'X.' It could be anything from "extra" to the association with cars similarly named like GTO, XL or XKE. The sound of GBX rung clean and unique in malt beverages and struck right on the target market."

Grain Belt's longtime advertising agency, Knox Reeves, came up with the blue and silver 12-

The GBX Malt Liquor media party in the Grain Belt brewery Friendship Room in June 1970. Looks like Lee Zanin of WWTC Radio (left) enjoyed a few. Also pictured, "GBX Girl" Carol Gheammaghami, Wally Green of WCCO and Paul Ewing, brewery communications sales.

and 16-oz. cans with embossed lettering that would appeal particularly to young males, along with advertising featuring racing and action themes, using the slogan "The New Brew for the New Breed." Commercials produced by Herb Pilhofer and vocalized by local singer Arne Fogel (whose youthful voice was known for commercials for Arctic Cat snowmobiles, the Embers restaurants and many other advertisers, plus a Minneapolis-based rock band called the Batch) hit the airwaves.

Promotions for the product kicked off with small airplanes flying over area beaches and other places carrying a tow that read "GBX Malt Liquor Is Here," with other aircraft skywriting "GBX." Colorful racing-themed (and later ski-themed) posters promoting GBX were given away at liquor outlets (a promotion very popular with the college student crowd). Four young women (dubbed "GBX Girls") were hired to promote the product in public, giving away GBX promotional items and sometimes serving free cups of the brew. A small fleet of Corvettes, painted in GBX insignia, cruised the Twin Cities and appeared at events. GBX sponsored races at Donnybrook Raceway in Brainerd, MN along with Union 76 gasoline (another name that was new to Minnesota). Blue GBX racing jackets became quite the fashion statement for young guys as well. It was the biggest promotional blitz for a new product ever done by Grain Belt, and it was incredibly successful, with sales going well beyond expectations—at least for a while.

1971 Minneapolis City Directory ad, featuring the Grain Belt family of products.

Aggressive Marketing

The company continued to aggressively promote its flagship Grain Belt brand as well, also with the use of promotional items to entice a younger crowd of drinkers while not alienating the older fans. Grain Belt T-shirts, jackets, tote bags, beach towels, lighters, key rings, wastebaskets, lamps, radios and other items were sold or given away.

Furthering its appeal to young people, Grain Belt was served at the very first Minnesota Renaissance Festival in 1971, then called the Renaissance Art Fair, at "Ye Auld Grain Belt Pub." Grain Belt sponsored radio and TV coverage of Minnesota North Stars hockey games and was served at Metropolitan Sports Center, where the home games were played. North Stars broadcaster Al Shaver made public appearances on behalf of Grain Belt in a role similar to what Billy Martin had in the 1960s, and wrote a "Hockey Talk" column for the company newsletter, the Grain Belt Diamond.

Grain Belt billboards continued to attract attention and industry awards. There was "The schooner the better" (a glass schooner filled with Grain Belt, with foam spilling off the top), "Grain Belt 6 – Thirst 0" (six empty cans of Grain Belt), "Rib tickler" (Grain Belt with barbecued ribs), even a nod to "Women's Liberation" (featuring feminine-looking hands with polished nails cradling a mug of Grain Belt) and many other examples. But one of the most popular and memorable billboards featured a large green hand hoisting a foaming mug of Grain Belt, with the slogan, "Ho! Ho! Ho!" implying that even the Jolly Green Giant (another Minnesota icon) drinks Grain Belt beer.

Ho! Ho! Ho! The "Green Giant" Grain Belt billboard proved so popular, the company turned it into a giveaway poster in 1973.

In the spring of 1973, the company held a "Create Your Own Grain Belt Billboard" contest. The grand prize, a 1973 Kayot Capri 23' motor home, was won by 25-year-old Mike Phillips of Burnsville—better known as WDGY morning disc jockey Charlie Van Dyke. Grain Belt just happened to be a major advertiser on WDGY. Winning entries were not released to the public, and it is unclear if any of the ideas were used on any Grain Belt billboards.

In June 1973, Minnesota's drinking age was lowered from 21 to 18, a trend that was happening in many states in the wake of the Vietnam War, where young men who were not allowed to drink at home were still forced to fight and die on the other side of the world for their country.

Grain Belt welcomed the lower drinking age, with Ed Koller, vice-president of marketing, stating in an article in the June 1973 Grain Belt Diamond, "Grain Belt's advertising program throughout the years has always been directed to the 18-49 year old market… The future of any company, particularly ours in the beer industry, relies heavily on the young adult market, namely 18-34 year olds.

"The 18 year old will contribute to a plus in sales. We do everything possible to encourage their call brand to be 'Grain Belt'…We would also like to encourage this group to visit our

New Grain Belt Premium can, introduced in 1973.

Grain Belt on draft was a specialty at Twin Cities area Shakey's Pizza Parlors.

facilities in Minneapolis and learn more about our product. Invite them to Grain Belt."

Also in 1973, promotion of Grain Belt Premium, the "beer of exceptional quality," was revived. Grain Belt Premium became available in non-returnable clear bottles, and also in an exclusively designed 12 ounce can with a solid gold background with the word "Premium" prominent, distinguishing it from regular Golden Grain Belt. A radio jingle sang, "You'll love Grain Belt, the Premium beer, the water's why…that's why!" in commercials that also referenced the old "diamond clear" and "it's been a long time a-brewing" slogans. Grain Belt Bock beer also made a comeback, on a seasonal basis.

Meanwhile, as sales of GBX Malt Liquor dropped off after an initially strong launch, the brand was phased out as Grain Belt entered a deal to distribute Country Club Malt Liquor, made by the Pearl Brewing Company of San Antonio, Texas.

Troubled Brewing Waters

Despite good marketing and Grain Belt's continued status as the top selling beer in Minnesota, the company's troubles were mounting. Among other things, regional breweries were rapidly losing ground to the big national breweries, namely Anheuser-Busch, Schlitz, Pabst and Miller, which had recently become a subsidiary of tobacco giant Phillip Morris. Grain Belt, Hamm's and Schmidt all saw losses in the early 1970s. Schmidt and its St. Paul brewery were sold to the G. Heileman Brewing Company of La Crosse, Wisconsin in 1972, and there were talks of a merger between Grain Belt and Hamm's, until the U. S. Justice Department threatened to block such a merger.

The national brewers continued to grow at the expense of the regionals. Their advertising budgets alone were often equal to the entire gross sales revenue of companies like Grain Belt, making it difficult to keep pace. They also engaged in deep-discounting of their beers on a retail level, making it all the more difficult to compete on price. While Grain Belt sales still held 24 percent of Minnesota's beer market, compared with Budweiser at only ten percent and Miller at less than two percent, the heavyweights of the industry were determined to change that by any means necessary.

In May 1972, five years after it took over management of the Storz Brewing Company, Grain Belt Breweries, Inc. announced it would be closing the Omaha brewery within 60 days, citing financial losses at the operation, which they blamed on undercutting by Anheuser-Busch of St. Louis and Schlitz of Milwaukee, in collusion with three local distributors.

In November 1972, Grain Belt filed suit against A-B and Schlitz as well as the three Omaha-based beer distributors in United States Federal Court, Nebraska District, claiming the larger breweries engaged in a price fixing scheme to monopolize business and restrain free trade with their marketing practices in Nebraska and Iowa, resulting in the closure of the Omaha brewery. Anheuser-Busch counter-sued, and eventually Grain Belt settled out of court with both breweries. Meanwhile, Grain Belt's earnings dropped from $198,000 or 20 cents a share in the third quarter of 1971 to $20,000 or two cents a share in the third quarter of 1972.

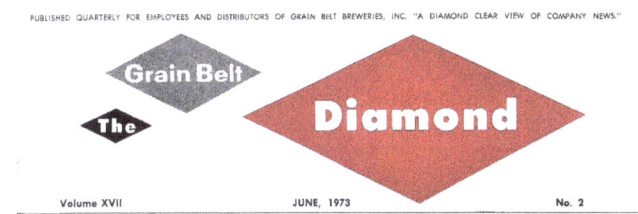

Frank Kiewel had stepped aside as company president at the beginning of the decade, and was named Chairman of the Board while Lee Birdsong assumed the role of Grain Belt president. But when Birdsong resigned from the company in August 1972, Kiewel was named CEO, and was credited with reviving morale throughout the company with his leadership.

On September 30, 1973, Frank Kiewel retired from Grain Belt after 40 years of service, but remained on the board of

Frank Kiewel and Grain Belt Park, 1973.

directors and as consultant to the company. Gerald Myer had been named president of the company five months earlier, in April 1973. A plaque was installed at the entrance of Grain Belt Park, in honor of Frank Kiewel for his contributions to the company and in the building of the park.

Grain Belt billboards and print ads from the late 1960s and early 1970s.

Take our best with the wurst.

Create a frank 'n stein.

One pitcher is worth 1,000 words.

Grain Belt 6   Thirst 0

For pizza sake.

It cuts the mustard.

The first, period.

The ahhhh couple.

Sure glad I fondue.

BREAKAWAY!

Feast and foremost.

The schooner the better.

MINNESOTA TWINS SCHEDULE 1972

The Best Things In Life Are Here

In 1974, competition was increasing all the more with the introduction of Washington-based Olympia and Pabst's popular-priced Red, White & Blue beer to Minnesota. Grain Belt meanwhile purchased the rights to an old 1920s pop song called "The Best Things In Life Are Free" and introduced a new advertising campaign, "The Best Things In Life Are Here," as a tribute to "Good Friends, Good Times and Grain Belt Beer" in commercial jingles sung by St. Paul native Mary MacGregor (who had a national hit single a few years later called "Torn Between Two Lovers") as well as the nationally-known Anita Kerr singers, plus a country-flavored version sung by Ray King. Imaging conjured up the good life in Minnesota and the surrounding region, and how Grain Belt beer fit into it all. There was a "Best Things In Life Are Here" contest, and the radio campaign won first place in a Brewers' Association of America competition that included entrants from thirty breweries nationwide.

The objectives of the ad campaign were outlined in the March 1974 Grain Belt Diamond. "(1) We have to relate our massage and image to the medium to heavy beer drinking males 18 to 34 years old. (2) We have to relate Grain Belt goes with the leisure hour activities relative to the geographic area. (3) We will portray that Grain Belt is the friendly beer. (4) We will maintain and provide the leadership image. (5) And last but certainly not least, Grain Belt is the premium quality beer."

Grain Belt greatly improved the look of its 12-can packs, going from corrugated boxes with limited colors to full color chipboard cartons. The new cartons for Golden Grain Belt featured an artist's rendering of Grain Belt Park with the brewery in the background, while Grain Belt Premium had a classy look with a depiction of an etched mirror with the Premium insignia. White Label, Hauenstein, Storz Triumph and Storz Premium also received new colorful 12-pack designs.

Grain Belt continued to be the best seller in Minnesota and its drinkers were fiercely loyal to the brand, with some even painting Grain Belt insignia on their ice houses on Minnesota lakes during ice fishing season, some of which were pictured in the Grain Belt Diamond. In the summer, Grain Belt Park continued to be a popular local attraction, hosting a variety of events

New 12-pack can cartons for Grain Belt Golden and Premium, introduced in 1974.

and multiple daily brewery tours.

Despite the marketing efforts and the local brand loyalty, Grain Belt's problems were mounting, especially with Frank Kiewel no longer at the helm. In addition to the new competitive challenges from the big national brewers, the United States economy was in the midst of a deep recession in 1974 with seemingly out-of-control inflation and an energy crisis that ultimately affected the cost of everything, including the materials needed to make beer and packaging, along with transportation. The big brewers could absorb these costs better than Grain Belt could, putting the company at an even greater disadvantage. In addition, the quality of the product was starting to slip, as Grain Belt began adding a preservative to its beers, giving them what was described by some as a "slightly burnt" taste and "weird" aftertaste, further turning off consumers. Sales were on the decline, and so was Grain Belt's stock price. Shareholders were getting impatient.

In his 1974 year-end message to employees and distributors, Grain Belt president Gerald N. Meyer expressed hope that "Grain Belt (will) come back strong in 1975" and that "The upcoming year is extremely crucial to all Grain Belt people. We have the necessary ingredients, so now everyone – each employee and each distributor – must give the 100% effort required. Then 1975 will be a truly joyous year."

Meanwhile, a man named Irwin Jacobs was taking advantage of the declining stock price by buying up as many shares of it as he could.

The Fountain Runs Dry

Grain Belt and its longtime agency Knox Reeves kicked off 1975 with the launching of a new ad campaign, "The Best Tastin' Beer Is Here," as a follow-up to the previous year's "Best Things In Life" campaign. Table tents with that theme appeared early on in area restaurants, as billboards, television and radio commercials and merchandise was prepared. But there would soon be drastic changes at the brewery.

The company was hurting. It had steadily lost money over the past several years, losing $158,839 on sales of $29.8 million in 1974, according to newspaper articles from the time.

As Grain Belt struggled to remain relevant, let alone expand market share in a rapidly-changing industry, a man by the name of Irwin Jacobs, vice-president of the Northwestern Bag Corporation, formally offered to purchase Grain Belt Breweries, Inc. in the spring of 1975. He had bought over $81,000 in company stock in February, making him the company's largest shareholder. The 36-year-old businessman offered $4.1 million for the company, about $4.70 per share.

Many of the employees, wholesalers and some stockholders were alarmed by the proposition. Jacobs had absolutely no experience in the brewing industry but he did have a wheeler-dealer reputation. From the beginning there were rumors that he would simply liquidate the company. Jacobs, with his business-like charm, tried to calm everyone's fears.

"I've got no intention of doing anything other than running this company as a brewery," he was quoted as telling everyone at a stockholders meeting in a Minneapolis Tribune article. "I've got no intention of closing it or liquidating it. I believe that, with the right approach, it can survive."

At that rather volatile stockholders meeting, the proposition was met with skepticism. Some objected outright, others suggested that the sale should be delayed for at least eighteen months. But when it came to a vote, the sale of Grain Belt Breweries, Inc. was approved overwhelmingly, with 613,908 shares for and 163,075 against, officially making it a privately-held company with Irwin Jacobs as owner, chairman and chief executive officer.

There were promises on the part of Jacobs that he would breathe new life into the company. "Irwin is devoting his full time to the future of Grain Belt," proclaimed the July 1975 Grain Belt

Diamond, which featured a portrait of Irwin on its cover. But Irwin Jacobs wasn't really interested in running a brewery. He was more interested in redeveloping that valuable real estate near the Mississippi River.

The Grain Belt Guys

As Grain Belt's board of directors contemplated the offer from Irwin Jacobs, a decision was made to sever the company's 20-year relationship with its advertising agency Knox Reeves, and move to New York-based Batton, Barto, Durstine & Osborne, Inc. (BBD&O), which the company had also done business with in the past along with locally-based Knox Reeves. The "Best Tastin' Beer" campaign was scuttled, and a whole new campaign was introduced with the slogan "Thirst Things First," featuring three fun-loving beer drinking buddies known as The Grain Belt Guys. It would be the final ad campaign from Grain Belt Breweries, Inc, now a division of I.J. Enterprises.

Portraying the Grain Belt Guys were three California-based actors: Renny Roker, Archie Hahn and Mark Giardino. The three men had appeared separately in other TV commercials and had bit parts in a few TV shows and movies. Roker also had a recurring role in the CBS comedy series Gomer Pyle, USMC a few years earlier and before that worked for singer Nat King Cole, and Hahn made a few appearances as one of Oscar's poker playing buddies on ABC's The Odd Couple. The guys were flown in, and the commercials were shot in Minnesota.

The Grain Belt Guys: Archie Hahn, Renny Roker and Mark Giardino.

The roving Grain Belt Guys, wearing big red Grain Belt diamond logos on their shirts, would rescue other guys from uncomfortable situations in a series of humorous commercials by calling out "Pssst—Hey you! Let's have a Grain Belt!" In one of the commercials, for example, the Grain Belt Guys crash a wedding and call a nervous bridegroom away for a beer just as he's about to tie the knot. In another, the Guys lure a bored young man, who is accompanying his snobbish rich boss and boss's wife, away from his seat at the opera for a Grain Belt in the middle of an aria.

Other commercials were filmed at various spots around the Twin Cities area, including the IDS Building (then the only modern skyscraper in Minneapolis), Naegele Outdoor Advertising Company (Grain Belt was one of that company's biggest clients), a barber shop and at the beach. The Guys were happy non-conformist partiers who confounded the conformist snobs in the commercials, and as it would turn out, in real life as well.

While the commercials undoubtedly played on youth appeal, at a time when states including Minnesota were lowering their drinking ages to 18, the actors portraying the Grain Belt Guys were all hovering around age 30, so they themselves weren't all that young, but not all that old either. A perfect fit to attract the targeted 18-34 year old male beer drinker.

In addition to commercials, the Guys were brought in for personal appearances around Minnesota in the summer of 1975, including the Minneapolis Aquatennial, where they rode the Grain Belt float and waved to enthusiastic spectators in the Torchlight Parade.

According to an article in the October 1975 Grain Belt Diamond, "Everywhere the Grain Belt Guys went they were recognized by thousands of fans…The three Grain Belt Guys enjoy their role and popularity in the Upper Midwest. Every place they would go they would hear "Psssst, hey you" from thousands of fans. They're neat guys and are helping to sell Grain Belt Beer."

The Grain Belt Guys were even parodied in a Richard Guindon cartoon panel published in the July 2, 1975 Minneapolis Tribune. In it, the Guys are drunk, sick and in the gutter, while a young boy asks his mother as they pass by, "What's the matter with the Grain Belt guys, Mom?"

But not everyone was a fan of the Grain Belt Guys. The United Presbyterian Church filed an official complaint with the Federal Communications Commission as well as Grain Belt owner Irwin Jacobs over the wedding commercial, finding the church setting in which the Guys do their "Pssst—Hey you! Let's have a Grain Belt" routine sacrilegious. The Presbyterian organization also complained that a Grain Belt radio spot featured religious music, but Grain Belt officials insisted it was "soul music."

The opera commercial also drew protest, this time from a culture lady from the Twin Cities Metropolitan Arts Alliance who complained that particular spot seemed to "reinforce the notion that only rich, society people can go and enjoy the arts" and that "there could have been a lot of other ways to make the commercial without putting down not only the opera but the people who attend it," she was quoted in the Minneapolis Star. Others complained the commercials promoted youth drinking.

Other Promotions

The advertising budget for Grain Belt was indeed increased under Irwin Jacobs. As a counterpart to the Grain Belt Guys, the company introduced two women, Mary Jo Philipp and Elaine Hall, billed as the Grain Belt Gals. Elaine Hall had previously worked for the company as a "GBX Girl." The Grain Belt Gals made appearances on TV and around Grain Belt's marketing area, handing out booklets of recipes that include beer and demonstrating some of these recipes, plus other promotions for Grain Belt.

L-R Mary Jo Philipp, Bobby Riggs and Elaine Hall

Bobby Riggs with the Grain Belt Gals

The company also hired middle-aged professional tennis player Bobby Riggs, known for the infamous "Battle of the Sexes" match with Billie Jean King, as a good will ambassador for Grain Belt, similar to what Billy Martin had done years earlier. Bobby signed autographs for the public and schmoozed with the Grain Belt Gals and female tour guides at the brewery in personal appearances, all in good fun.

Grain Belt expanded its merchandise line to consumers, with items such as clothing, belt buckles, patches, beach towels, plastic mugs, can coolers, glassware, nostalgic Stanley and Albert mugs, pool table overhead lamps, and other items. The company gave away reprints of the infamous 1930s "Girl in the Barley Field" posters, an image that was considered scandalous in the '30s but quaint in the '70s.

Grain Belt attempted to further solidify its "hip" factor with young people, sponsoring showings of the irreverent British comedy show "Monty Python's Flying Circus" on Twin Cities Public Television station KTCA-TV Channel 2. (In those days, sponsor tags on Public Television consisted simply of a mention of the company name at the beginning and ending of the show with no logos or advertising of any kind.)

Meanwhile, Irwin Jacobs was shopping around the Grain Belt labels to rival breweries.

Pulling the Plug

On December 1, 1975, a Grain Belt spokesman, citing disappointing sales and continued loss of revenue, announced that Grain Belt would be selling its name and assets to the G. Heileman Brewing Company of La Crosse, Wisconsin, pending U.S. Justice Department approval, and the brewery would be closing at the end of the year. Heileman owned and operated the rival Jacob Schmidt brewery in St. Paul.

With the blessing of the Justice Department's Anti-Trust Division, which a few years earlier had blocked a proposed merger between Grain Belt and Hamm's, Irwin Jacobs sold the Grain Belt labels, inventories and wholesale organization to Heileman for $4 million, a little less than what he paid for the entire company eight months earlier.

The last brewery operating in Minneapolis folded at the end of 1975, with the remaining product shipped out in early 1976. Some 400 jobs were lost. Production of Grain Belt Golden, Grain Belt Premium, Hauenstein and the Storz brands moved to Heileman's La Crosse, Wisconsin and St. Paul plants. White Label was sold off along with a few third-tier Heileman brands (including Gluek) to the Cold Spring Brewing Company of Cold Spring, Minnesota. The Diamond Wells Fountain, running continuously in front of the Grain Belt brewery since June 1963, was shut off for good.

What remained of the Diamond Wells Fountain at Grain Belt Park after the brewery closed. A dry pipe in the middle of some cemented boulders.

House of Heileman

The G. Heileman Brewing Company of La Crosse, Wisconsin for years had been a struggling regional brewery whose primary brand was Old Style Lager, but in the 1960s the decision was made to grow the company through the acquisition of other regional breweries and brands in response to increasingly fierce competition from the big national brewers that was driving so many of those smaller brewers out of business. Heileman had acquired the Blatz label in 1969 (beating out, ironically, Grain Belt and Schmidt who had also bid on it), and in 1972 the company bought up the assets of Associated Brewing Company, parent of the Jacob Schmidt Brewing Company in St. Paul as well as other breweries and labels. Under Heileman, little had changed in the day-to-day operations of Schmidt, arguably Grain Belt's fiercest rival.

On February 12, 1976, the G. Heileman Brewing Company ran an ad in Minnesota newspapers headlined GRAIN BELT FOREVER, with "A pledge to all beer drinkers from the House of Heileman" by company president Russell G. Cleary.

Grain Belt became a second-tier brand in the vast House of Heileman, dominated in Minnesota by old arch-rival Schmidt.

"We are particularly happy to welcome Grain Belt, one of the country's great beers, into the House of Heileman family. We have hired many Grain Belt people, including two Grain Belt brewmasters. We will continue to brew this great beer in the Twin Cities.

"The House of Heileman now brews and sells more beer in Minnesota than any other brewer. We are beer people, first, last and always. Your support has made us #1. Since 1853 we have been brewing beers we can be proud of and we are now proud to add Grain Belt to the growing list of America's finest quality beers brewed by the House of Heileman. We consider Grain Belt to be a brand that will grow and prosper, and one that provides a golden opportunity for Heileman and for the Grain Belt wholesalers.

"To the loyal beer drinkers of Minnesota who made Grain Belt a top seller in the state, Heileman pledges, GRAIN BELT FOREVER."

Grain Belt loyalists were skeptical. Grain Belt, the Minneapolis beer, would now be brewed at the Heileman-owned Jacob Schmidt brewery in St. Paul, Grain Belt's arch-rival, as well as Heileman's Old Style plant in La Crosse, Wisconsin.

The look of Grain Belt changed. Early Grain Belt packaging under Heileman was similar to the old, with bottle labels and new crimped-steel cans that looked similar but with duller colors. But in

The new look of Grain Belt under the House of Heileman.

the summer of 1976, the Grain Belt labels underwent a complete makeover, with a redesigned Grain Belt diamond logo on a white background with gold and black trim, featuring the House of Heileman logo. The slogan "From Perfect Brewing Water" was carried over from the old design, albeit without the fountain.

In addition to the new label design, Grain Belt fans believed (although Heileman denied it) that the beer inside was not the same, that it had become a watered-down, bland-tasting generic swill that was the same brew put into bottles and cans of other lesser brands in the Heileman portfolio. Grain Belt sales rapidly fell after the move to Heileman, which didn't bother the company too much, as many former Grain Belt fans switched to Heileman's Schmidt, Old Style, Blatz or Special Export.

In early 1977, Grain Belt and Grain Belt Premium began to be packaged in aluminum cans for the first time, with a new "stay-tab" top, replacing the old tear-off pull tabs that had been banned in Minnesota (but continued to be used in Wisconsin and other states) due to environmental concerns. In 1978, the slogan "Go with the Grain" was introduced, and the brand was promoted by WCCO Radio afternoon personality Steve Cannon.

In 1981, Grain Belt Light was introduced to the product line, after Heileman came out victorious in a lawsuit by the Miller Brewing Company over the rights to use the name "Light" in beer brands (Miller contended it infringed on their own "Lite" brand). The slogan was, "Now you can have your light beer and taste it too."

Grain Belt became a less significant player in the market (although it did retain at least some of its loyal following), and many attribute it to the hostility that had existed between Grain Belt and Schmidt going way back. While Grain Belt had generally cordial relations with Hamm's, the rivalry with Schmidt was much more intense. Heileman's local sales director, N.G. (Poley) LaPage, was a Schmidt man all the way, beginning his

WCCO Radio personality Steve Cannon promoted Grain Belt in 1978.

career in the accounting department at Schmidt back in 1948. He was known for chasing Grain Belt out of area bars, having his salesmen throw money at saloon owners for their loyalty (as the Grain Belt people also did), and secretly replacing Grain Belt signs with Schmidt signs. He would secure the beer drinking public's loyalty to Schmidt by going into bars and buying rounds of "The Brew That Grew With the Great Northwest" for the patrons. Grain Belt and Schmidt distributors and route drivers were known for sabotaging each other's kegs with machine oil and swizzle sticks.

The Schmidt people had won the battle in Minnesota's beer wars, essentially taking Grain Belt as their P.O.W. There was speculation that Heileman only wanted it to eliminate competition and keep it out of the hands of someone who might really revitalize the brand and go after Schmidt (which Heileman steadfastly denied). Much of whatever revenue Grain Belt generated was diverted to promote Schmidt and the other first-tier Heileman brands, with Grain Belt receiving less promotion as the years went by and as sales continued to decline. From 1976, when Heileman took over Grain Belt, to 1986, Grain Belt production went from 800,500 barrels to 64,000 barrels and continued to decline significantly, hitting 21,500 barrels in 1991, when the brand was finally sold.

Meanwhile in Minneapolis

At the old Grain Belt brewery, a week-long auction began on May 10, 1976, liquidating the former company of almost everything that could be moved. Vats, copper brew kettles almost 20 feet in diameter, flow meters, pneumatic butterfly valves, steel fire doors, office equipment, promotional materials, some 5,000 unused 12 oz. Grain Belt and Grain Belt Premium cans that never made it to the canning line, and even vintage beer bottles from a display case in the brewery were sold to the highest bidder. Also included was brand new equipment that had just been shipped to the brewery but was never installed.

Most of the bidders were scrap dealers buying up the metal equipment. When it was over, about all that was left was some stainless steel storage tanks, some broken-down machinery and the ornamental iron staircase that wound its way through

The shuttered, and forlorn, Grain Belt brewery in Minneapolis.

The old tour center at Grain Belt Park, boarded up. The red diamond mural on the brewery was fading away, revealing an older mural with bottles from the 1960s, in this picture from the 1990s.

the brewhouse, which some of the scrap dealers also had their eye on.

In the aftermath of Grain Belt's closure, some 400 employees, with the exception of two brewmasters, a supervisor and nine salesmen who were hired by Heileman, were terminated. Forty learned later that they were losing their pensions because of a closure clause in their contracts agreed to when Grain Belt's demise seemed unimaginable.

Irwin Jacobs vehemently denied that he had purchased Grain Belt to liquidate it, claiming that in the mere eight months he had owned the company, he did absolutely everything he could possibly do to ensure its survival. The company was in such bad shape, he insisted, that even a genius like him couldn't save it.

Wheeler-dealer Jacobs, meanwhile, had plans to redevelop the riverfront property where the Grain Belt complex stood. The Minneapolis Industrial Development Commission had asked the City Council to consider buying the fifteen-acre site to serve as a foreign trade zone. While the city was "studying" the proposal, Jacobs quickly lost patience. Bulldozers were on site, and in a Minneapolis Tribune article from June 24, 1976 headlined "Grain Belt building may be smashed," Jacobs said, "I've been patient, and have given the city plenty of time to take a position. I'm not trying to blackmail anybody, but we've already got the rear of the building open and I can't afford to stop now," adding that demolition of the Grain Belt brewhouse will probably take a month.

The bulldozers had already taken out part of a wing on the north side of the building when his plan was abruptly halted. Little did he, nor city officials likely realize the rabid interest the community had in the old buildings. Northeast Minneapolis residents, preservationists, historians and even local business owners and politicians engaged in a grassroots effort to save the brewery, spearheaded by community activist Jeanette May.

The thought of the beautiful, historic brewhouse being smashed to rubble was appalling to many. To this day, people with interest in Minneapolis history are angered by the demolition of the old Metropolitan building in downtown Minneapolis, which was destroyed by short-sighted city officials in an urban renewal project in the early 1960s, as well as other historic structures.

This time around, community activists weren't going to let go of the Grain Belt brewery—even if it meant standing in front of the bulldozers.

To the surprise and chagrin of Jacobs, Jeanette May and her troops won over the City Council. The site was declared a historic landmark in 1977 and the demolition permit Jacobs had long sought was denied. Jacobs made further attempts to raze the brewery, which were again denied. This left him in the unfortunate position of having to pay taxes on property he had no use for, for years to come.

Finally, in the late 1980s, Jacobs offered to give the brewhouse to the city with a number of stipulations, including having it pay for the utilities of the other buildings on the site, which Jacobs had been renting out, and bearing the responsibility of cleaning up the various environmental hazards in the building, such as asbestos, and PCBs. The city turned down the offer but eventually agreed to buy the entire site, including the buildings being rented out, for $4.8 million.

(Some 30 years later, on April 10, 2019, Irwin Jacobs died along with his ailing wife in a murder-suicide at his home in a Minneapolis suburb.)

Developers were encouraged to come up with plans to redevelop the brewhouse and over the years there were many interesting ones, including an aquarium and marina complex, studios for video and movie production, Shakespearean stages, museums, microbreweries, manufacturing facilities, a Radisson Hotel conference center and others, but paying for the renovation had always been a sticking point. The old, outdated structure was rapidly decaying, and along with the oddball Victorian-era architecture, renovation costs were too prohibitive for most developers. There were holes in the floor 20 feet in diameter where the multi-story copper brew kettles used to be. Demolition remained a real possibility.

The Nicollet Island Sign

Amazingly, through all the changes the Grain Belt brand had gone through, including falling out of favor with the beer drinking public, the big 1940s era Grain Belt "bottle cap" neon sign located on Nicollet Island on the Mississippi River near the Hennepin Avenue Bridge facing downtown Minneapolis was still standing, although the lights on it went dark years ago.

The Eastman Family of Minneapolis owned the property where the sign stood, and in 1983, they first approached the G. Heileman Brewing Company about financing the re-lighting of

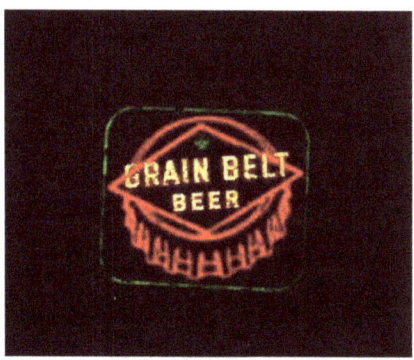

The Nicollet Island Grain Belt sign at day and night.

the big sign. Heileman, which owned Grain Belt but wasn't particularly interested in promoting it, opposed the idea, and suggested the outdated logo be trashed and replaced with an updated logo, or a sign promoting the more-favored Schmidt brand, or that other alterations be made.

But the Eastmans, along with the Minneapolis Heritage Preservation Commission, continued to lobby for full restoration and finally, on May 24, 1989, as the summer beer drinking season kicked off, the Grain Belt sign on Nicollet Island was lit up again, with Heileman picking up most of the cost of the restoration. SignCrafters restored the sign that was originally built by Naegele Outdoor, and everything on the sign had to be replaced, including all the wiring, 800 feet of neon tubing and 1,400 incandescent light bulbs in the lettering.

A crowd of about 200 gathered to see the re-lighting on that warm, almost-summer evening. The neon surrounding the diamond, the cap and the border came on, and the incandescent-lit lettering was supposed to flash in individual letters G-R-A-I-N B-E-L-T and the full word BEER, but the G and the A didn't light up in the first couple of cycles. Nonetheless the crowd applauded in excitement, and the whole thing lit up as intended after a couple of cycles.

But before long, there were problems. After a few months of running, some of the letters weren't lighting up, some of the neon also wasn't lighting and the electric bill to power the thing was very high. Another restoration was done in 1992, but the problems continued and lighting on the sign was shut down again in 1996. It would be more than twenty years before it would be lit up again.

The fall of House of Heileman

The G. Heileman Brewing Company continued to grow rapidly into the 1980s, primarily through acquisitions of other breweries and brands. By 1981 they were the fourth largest brewer in the country and the fastest-growing of all, and by 1986 they owned and operated twelve breweries in eleven states along with over 100 brand names. They also diversified into baking and other industries. On the other hand they were facing even more intense cut-throat competition from the big national brewers as the overall pie got smaller and consumers became more fickle, with beer sales declining. Plus, with all the regional labels they owned, they didn't bother to expand marketing beyond the original regions for

The G. Heileman Brewing Company was riding high when this 1986 annual report came out. Then the bottom fell out.

those brands and had no national brand, even as they became a national brewer. Nonetheless, they were still looking good in 1986.

Then in 1987, in a strange turn of events, Australian corporate raider Alan Bond, who controlled roughly half of the beer business in that country, made a hostile takeover bid for the G. Heileman Brewing Company. The company tried to fight it off, but Bond took over in a leveraged buyout, using junk bonds for the purchase. Soon after, Bond's worldwide business empire collapsed. Heileman closed several of its breweries including the Jacob Schmidt brewery in St. Paul in 1989, and in January 1991, the company filed bankruptcy. Production of Grain Belt, Schmidt and Hauenstein moved to La Crosse.

A group of investors raised funds to purchase the St. Paul brewery from Heileman in late 1991, just as the company was preparing to liquidate, with the intention of re-hiring the workers and re-opening the brewery under a new entity, Minnesota Brewing Company. The new company also purchased the Grain Belt labels from Heileman.

Meanwhile, the G. Heileman Brewing Company was bought by a private equity firm in 1994, which then sold it in 1996 to the Stroh Brewery Company, which owned St. Paul's other brewery, the former Hamm's plant. Then Stroh itself went out of business in 1999, the La Crosse brewery closed and the remaining Heileman assets went to other companies.

Grain Belt, against the odds, would make a comeback in the 1990s.

Depiction of the Schmidt Brewery in St. Paul, MN on a 1970s postcard.

Minnesota Brewing Company

From the ashes of Heileman in St. Paul rose Minnesota Brewing Company. When Heileman closed the old Jacob Schmidt brewery on West 7th Street, moving all production to its La Crosse, Wisconsin plant, the St. Paul neighborhood, and many Minnesotans, were upset. The brewery had been a big part of the neighborhood for so many decades, employing generations of residents. There was still a market for locally-produced product that supported local jobs.

With that idea in mind, St. Paul businessman Bruce Hendry, along with a group of other investors, purchased the former Schmidt brewery from Heileman, with some government assistance, in 1991. The new entity was called Minnesota Brewing Company, a name that sounded a lot like Minneapolis Brewing Company. When the brewery finally reopened months after the sale was finalized, the company started calling back its union workers on a seniority basis.

Hendry and company wanted to also buy back the Schmidt brand from Heileman but the La Crosse-based brewer didn't want to part with it, at least not without a hefty price. Heileman offered up Grain Belt at a much more modest price, and the Hendry group accepted.

The first beer the company released, called Landmark, turned up in liquor stores in December 1991 with an old fashioned depiction of the former Schmidt brewery etched in gold on a white background on the label, with the name Landmark in large red letters above it. The company had so much confidence in its new brand as the official flagship product, that the giant neon letters spelling out Schmidt above the brewery were taken down (and eventually destroyed), replaced with a cheaper-looking, unlit "Landmark" sign, a move that proved to be a major blunder. The brand flopped.

Grain Belt Premium started to appear shortly thereafter in early 1992 with Grain Belt Golden following on a more limited basis. A decision was made to make Premium, rather than Golden, as the main brand in the Grain Belt product line, although both brands would be produced. Premium came in clear bottles and red and white aluminum cans that still resembled Heileman's version of Grain Belt Premium, but with a more "retro" logo. Golden came in brown bottles and in red and gold cans that more resembled earlier Grain Belt packaging, with some updates to the label. Grain Belt Light and Premium Light were also released, featuring a blue Grain Belt diamond logo.

But with the old Schmidt/Heileman people still at the helm in the new company, Grain Belt was still treated as somewhat of a bastard stepchild, at least at first. Landmark was the "flagship" brand, and some Grain Belt advertising only carried the "Premium" name, as it was assumed there was stigma attached to "Grain Belt."

In the summer of 1992, Minnesota Brewing Company released another new brand called Pig's Eye Pilsner, named after an early inhabitant of St. Paul named Pierre Parrant, a.k.a. "Pig's Eye" Parrant. With an intriguing label design featuring a depiction of Parrant wearing an eye patch, and unusual and humorous commercials, Pig's Eye did attract a following. The company later released another product with an unusual name, McMahon's Original Irish Potato Ale (it did not taste like potatoes).

Minnesota Brewing also used some of the brewery's two million barrels a year capacity by contract brewing such products as Pete's Wicked Ale, Mike's Hard Lemonade and other microbrews and sweetened alcoholic beverages (sometimes referred to as "alco-pop").

Grain Belt rises again

To the surprise of practically everyone involved, sales of Grain Belt started taking off. There

Minnesota Brewing Company gave Grain Belt products a pre-Heileman, retro '70s look.

had been a renewed public interest in the brand with the re-lighting of the Nicollet Island sign in 1989, and with continued talks of renovation at the old Grain Belt brewery in Minneapolis. Minnesota Brewing Company, with far fewer labels than Heileman, put more promotion into Grain Belt than the brand had seen in years, and it was paying off. Emphasis was made on the fact that Grain Belt production had returned to Minnesota, and billboards around the Twin Cities for Grain Belt Premium carried the slogan, "Back Home Again. Better Than Ever."

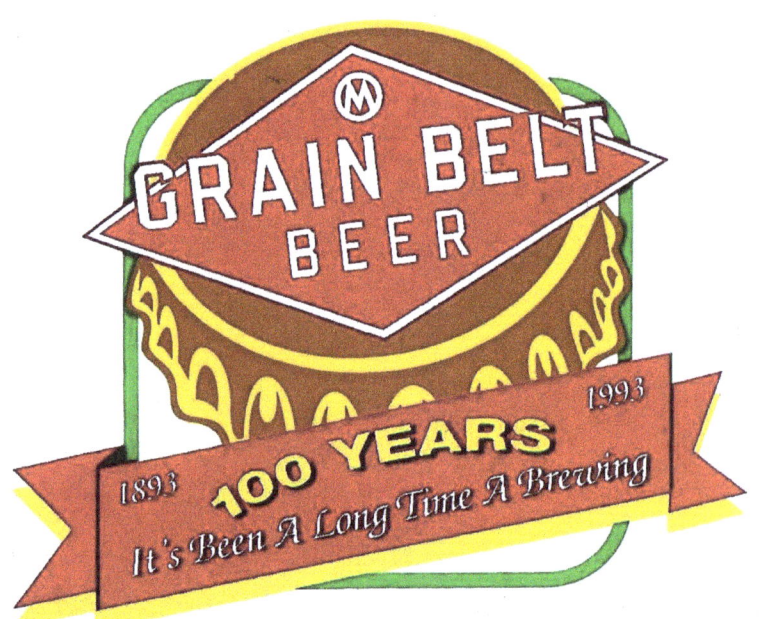

In 1993, Minnesota Brewing Company kicked off a Grain Belt 100th Anniversary promotion, commemorating the brand's introduction in 1893. A special logo, resembling the Nicollet Island bottle cap sign was created, and included the old slogan "It's been a long time a-brewing." There was a whole catalog of 100th Anniversary Grain Belt merchandise, featuring clothing, golf accessories, mugs, ceramic steins, clocks, coaster sets, belt buckles, decks of cards, pens and other things, plus the "crown jewel," a four-piece mirror set featuring past Grain Belt bottle labels bordering a red Grain Belt Premium diamond. Even Stanley and Albert made a brief comeback, with their images on a T-shirt and a couple of actors playing them in parades to promote the centennial celebration.

In October 1994, Grain Belt Premium won a Gold Medal Award for Best Lager at the Great American Beer Festival in Denver, Colorado. Minnesota Brewing Company put heavy promotion into this award, and sales of Grain Belt Premium skyrocketed to the point that supplies to distributors and retailers ran out in May 1995, just before Minnesota's fishing season opener. Maintenance on the canning line resulting in a shutdown of production during this time did not help.

Grain Belt promotions of the 1990s.

Minnesota Brewing Company tried to go beyond nostalgia in the promotion of Grain Belt Premium, targeting young, urban, nightclub-going Miller Genuine Draft drinkers with slogans such as "Have a Premo Night." Ultimately nostalgia would prevail, however, as the term "retro" became popular with young adults in the 1990s and stuff from the mid-20th Century became "hip." The big sign outside the brewery might have still promoted Landmark, but Grain Belt Premium had become the flagship brand of Minnesota Brewing Company.

After Grain Belt sales had reached an all-time low of 21,500 barrels in 1991, the last year it was produced by Heileman, sales jumped by more than 25 percent in each of the following years, and by 1993 it was already outselling Schmidt as that brand faded away. After Grain Belt Premium won the Gold Medal at the Great American Beer Festival, sales shot up by a mind-boggling 92 percent in 1996, to 130,000 barrels, the most Grain Belt sold since the late 1970s.

Most of the emphasis was on Grain Belt Premium, but in 1998 the company revitalized original Golden Grain Belt (in brown rather than clear bottles) with a new black label design based on the 1930s Grain Belt labels, featuring a modern Grain Belt logo over a bottle cap

Upgraded 'retro" look for Golden Grain Belt in the late 1990s.

Amber Lager was the first (and only) brew of the Grain Belt Archive Series.

image, with the word "Golden," and the old slogan "The Friendly Beer" prominently in the design.

Minnesota Brewing even brought back GBX Malt Liquor for a time, first with a completely re-designed (and unrecognizable) label, then with the familiar blue and silver racing stripes that resembled the early 1970s cans, in 12 and 16 ounce sizes, although now all-aluminum with stay-tab tops.

In addition, to get in on the growing popularity of craft beers, Minnesota Brewing introduced the Grain Belt Archive Series, which they claimed were from "a recent discovery of recipes from the original Grain Belt Brewery," with a label using a graphic from the earliest Grain Belt labels of the 1890s and early 1900s. The first in the series was Amber Lager. Unfortunately, they never got beyond that one.

In 1998, Minnesota Brewing Company introduced a redesigned corporate logo, ditching the pine trees for a circular symbol with a letter M in the center that strongly resembled the old Minneapolis Brewing Company logo from a century earlier. Meanwhile, Grain Belt entered the Internet age when Minnesota Brewing Company put the grainbelt.com website online around this time as well.

Minnesota Brewing Goes Down

On the other end of 7th Street in St. Paul, Stroh, the Michigan-based brewer which operated the former Hamm's brewery (but didn't make Hamm's), had acquired what remained of the G. Heileman Brewing Company in 1996. The company decided to go after Grain Belt Premium with the revival of another old brand, Schmidt's City Club, also in clear bottles and with a "retro" label. But then that nearly 150-year-old company folded in 1999, and its St. Paul brewery closed, leaving Minnesota Brewing Company as the state's largest brewer and its plant the last of the big Twin Cities breweries still operating.

However, problems for Minnesota Brewing Company were mounting. Management had turned over by the late 1990s and sales were decreasing as the company made a number of marketing blunders. The brewery, with its two million barrel capacity, was too big and

Billboard outside the St. Paul brewery.

cumbersome for the operation that currently existed there, the equipment was becoming outdated, contracts to brew other products were expiring and not being renewed and debts were piling up.

In 1999, in an attempt to keep the company afloat and bring in new revenue, the decision was made by the parent holding company to start a new business on site, Gopher State Ethanol, to manufacture industrial-grade ethanol from grain. The state and federal governments offered subsidies in the manufacture of ethanol, and the profits could be used to keep the brewery afloat and keep the local jobs that the company was formed to bring back in the first place.

While the West Seventh Neighborhood wanted the brewery, they didn't want the ethanol plant, with the noise it made and the stench that came from it. Minnesota Brewing management tried to assure the residents that the plant was good for the neighborhood and that it will save the brewery jobs, as the complaints rolled in.

Gopher State Ethanol however was not bringing in enough revenue to keep the brewery afloat. The brewery took out a $5.4 million loan to buy new equipment to speed up production. But the opposite happened as the new equipment did not arrive on schedule and when it did, production had to be shut down for days to install it. Orders backed up and the debts continued to mount. Sales of Grain Belt slipped to about half of what they were at its 1996 peak, as other company brands also declined dramatically and local beer drinkers were either sticking with their corporate light beers or trying the new craft brews that were coming out.

At the beginning of 2002, Minnesota Brewing Company was drowning in debt of more than $17 million. The company requested a loan from the St. Paul City Council to keep the brewery afloat and save neighborhood jobs but the Council rejected the request, and Minnesota Brewing Company filed Chapter 11 bankruptcy.

The company continued to operate, treading on thin ice, until June 24, 2002 when Bremer Bank foreclosed and shut the brewery down. Employees were called to the brewery's tap room, were told the brewery was closing and that they had 30 minutes to collect their belongings and leave the property. Bottling lines were shut down in midstream and beer remained in various stages of production. Bremer Bank did not care and did not allow any employees to remain on the job to properly shut down and mothball the brewery. The old Schmidt brewery was now abandoned, Minnesota Brewing Company ceased to exist and Grain Belt, along with other Minnesota Brewing Company brands, was in limbo. Meanwhile, Gopher State Ethanol continued to operate.

New Life at Old Grain Belt

As Minnesota Brewing Company was suffering the woes that would lead to its demise, there were new signs of life at the old Grain Belt brewery in Northeast Minneapolis that had been shuttered for over two decades.

Irwin Jacobs, unable to tear down the buildings and redevelop the property, sold the property to the City, which put it in the hands of the Minneapolis Community Development Agency (MCDA). As the MCDA considered proposals from potential developers, crews began to clean up the exterior of the brewhouse in the mid 1990s, cleaning off decades of grime that gave the building a dark brown color, and stabilized the structure, to make sure the thing wouldn't end up falling down on its own after nearly a quarter century of neglect.

In the decade that the MCDA owned the property, potential developers were sought out who would do something useful with the

The 1990s brought renovations at the old Grain Belt Brewery.

former brewery, yet maintain its historic character and integrity. Would-be suitors of all stripes came up with ideas ranging from factories to studios to museums to microbreweries, only to get cold feet when confronted with the oddities of the structure, the numerous problems that accumulated after 25 years of dormancy and the costs associated with correcting all those problems. Many experts advised that that practical thing to do would be to just knock the thing down and build something new.

Meanwhile, other buildings on the Grain Belt property, including the office, warehouse, bottling house and keg house, were rented out for offices, artists' studios and the like.

Finally, in late 1999, the construction firm Ryan Companies stepped forward with a proposal to buy the grand old brewhouse and convert it into office space for RSP Architects, Ltd., with promises of retaining and preserving as much of the historic design as possible.

After months of discussion, paperwork, public hearings, bureaucratic nonsense and hand-wringing, the massive job of converting a late 19th Century brewery into a 21st Century office building began. First, every nook and cranny of the interior had to be sanitized with a solution of bleach and hot water to rid it of the left over yeast

The original Grain Belt Brewery became headquarters for RSP Architects in 2002.

residue that gave the entire interior a musty basement smell. Asbestos, lead paint and other hazardous materials also had to be removed. The slate roof was restored with slate shingles, even though it would have been a lot cheaper to use standard roofing. Some interior walls were demolished, along with some entrances and stairs that weren't up to current building code. The old fermenting tanks, remaining pieces of machinery and a mildew-stained "Grain Belt Guys" billboard were removed with cutting torches.

Plaster was scraped away from some walls and ceilings, revealing long-unseen brickwork, which was incorporated into the new interior. New windows were cut into brick facades. The brick, in turn, was recycled back into the building, filling in where needed. Wooden catwalks were built to connect the areas of the building where floors didn't match up from one section to the next. The centerpiece of the interior, the giant ornamental iron staircase with all the twists and turns, had to be taken out and rebuilt to bring it up to current building code. It would have cost far less to simply build new stairs, but the decision was made to spare no expense in preserving as much as possible of the historic structure. A glass elevator was installed in the giant holes in the floors that once held brew kettles. The project took over a year and $22 million to complete. The 200 employees of RSP Architects moved into their new home in February 2002.

Fittingly, RSP Architects was selected to design a new Pierre Bottineau Public Library on the grounds of the Grain Belt brewery, after voters approved of new library funding in a 2000 referendum, where the old Gasthaus/Grain Belt tour center was located by the brewery park. The buildings that made up the old tour center were originally a millwright shop and wagon shed for the brewery, built in the early 20th Century. The original Pierre Bottineau Library had been in a tiny storefront location blocks away.

As the renovation process began in early 2002, remnants of an 1890s-era ice house, where the original Minneapolis Brewing and Malting Company stored product in the days before electric refrigeration, was discovered. The blueprints for the new library were altered as a result, to preserve the footprint of the long-lost historic structure.

Remaining remnants of Grain Belt Park were taken out, including the wooden façade of the buildings, the non-functioning fountain, the remaining landscaping and several trees in the process. Bricks removed from the brewhouse during its renovation were recycled back into the new library. There was talk of rebuilding the fountain, but funds could only be raised for a much smaller replica.

The Grand Opening of the new Pierre Bottineau Library was on May 31, 2003. It was part of the Minneapolis Public Library system at the time of the opening, which was merged into the Hennepin County Library system in 2008.

The rehabilitation of the Grain Belt site in its entirety was finally completed in 2015, nearly 40 years after the brewery closed, as new apartment buildings, called The Grain Belt, located across Marshall Street from the brewery were opened, using the original Grain Belt office building as the office and recreation center for the apartments.

Renovation of the office building wasn't easy. There were leaks in the roof and the walls as well as other problems. But in the process of fixing it up, a skylight that had been covered by a newer roof was opened up, bringing outdoor light into the remodeled main floor. As much as could be preserved in the building was preserved, including the executive offices in the upper level, and the Friendship Room taproom in the basement.

Building of the 150-unit apartments next to the office building, in what had been the brewery's old parking lot, had to be delayed when it was discovered that remains of the foundation of the original John Orth Brewery, built in 1850 and demolished after the Minneapolis Brewing Company brewery was built, was buried underneath. Construction of the apartments commenced a little east of the lot, and a courtyard outlining the footprint of the Orth Brewery was put in.

And in St. Paul, the former Schmidt brewery sat dormant for a decade after Minnesota Brewing Company closed in 2002. The ethanol plant that was opened ostensibly to "save" the brewery closed in 2004. Finally, in 2012, renovations there began to convert that former brewery into the Schmidt Artists Lofts. The Landmark sign was taken down and neon letters spelling out Schmidt in its original 1950s logo font reappeared. The originals had been destroyed, but the blueprints were found, enabling their recreation. The Schmidt Artists Lofts had a public Grand Opening with a first annual German Fest on the grounds, on June 21, 2014. Thousands attended.

Inside the restored Grain Belt Brewery office building, 2018.

Grain Belt Moves to New Ulm

The year 2002 was likely the most topsy-turvy in the history of Grain Belt. In February, the old Grain Belt brewery in Minneapolis came back to life as the new headquarters of RSP Architects. In June, production of Grain Belt beer in St. Paul was halted as parent Minnesota Brewing Company was shut down and went out of business. Grain Belt disappeared from liquor stores and bars that summer as remaining supplies ran out. The brand's future was in limbo. A Miller or Anheuser-Busch or Coors wouldn't likely be interested in it, and it wouldn't quite be "Grain Belt" if it were brewed in another state anyway.

Two brewers in Minnesota did express interest in acquiring Grain Belt, however. The Summit Brewing Company of St. Paul and August Schell Brewing Company of New Ulm.

Summit was founded in 1986 by Mark Stutrud as a microbrewery. It had grown considerably in its fairly short history, and had just built a brand new facility, but it was still relatively small, its specialty was craft-style rather than mass-market beers, and at the time they didn't even have a canning line.

Schell was founded in New Ulm, Minnesota near the Cottonwood River in 1860, had stayed in the same family and was currently owned by a fifth generation Schell descendant, Ted Marti, and his wife Jodi. For years it operated as a small regional brewery that was overshadowed by the large regionals in the Twin Cities such as Grain Belt and Schmidt. Its main in-town competition was Hauenstein, which was acquired by Grain Belt after the New Ulm brewery down the street from Schell closed in 1969.

Schell was a rarity in that it was an old regional brewery that managed to stay in business in the face of so much national competition, when so many much larger and better-known breweries

died off. It was also the second-oldest family-owned brewery in the United States. In recent years, Schell had been doing better than the industry as a whole, with a brewery expansion, a new emphasis on specialty and craft beers, and an increasing share of sales in its marketing area.

In August 2002, two months after production ceased in St. Paul, the orphaned Grain Belt became part of the Schell family, the fourth company to make it since the original Minneapolis brewery shut down 27 years earlier. It was the biggest investment--and risk--in the company's 142-year history. The purchase made August Schell Brewing Company the largest brewery in Minnesota.

The Great Grain Belt Moving Party

As the new owner of Grain Belt, Ted Marti promised to maintain the brand's heritage, to invest more into promotion and to get young and old beer drinkers alike to be proud Grain Belt drinkers. Production of Grain Belt in New Ulm began in August, two months after production ceased in St. Paul, but to officially welcome the brand into the Schell family and

bring it back into the public eye, The Great Grain Belt Moving Party was scheduled for October 25, 2002 at the former Grain Belt Bottling House, a block over from the original Grain Belt brewery in Northeast Minneapolis. It would be a private party for industry VIPs, media and Grain Belt fans who signed up on the grainbelt.com website. There would be prizes, a polka band, displays of vintage Grain Belt memorabilia, salty snacks such as hard-boiled eggs, crackers, popcorn and pickled chicken gizzards (in the tradition of the "bar dinners" of decades past) and plenty of Grain Belt Premium, fresh-brewed in New Ulm, to wash it all down.

A scroll with the original recipe for Grain Belt Premium would be symbolically dropped into the bung hole of a large aluminum keg in the very building where Grain Belt beer was packaged decades ago and "moved" to its new home in New Ulm. There was an initial plan to bring the whole party to New Ulm by charter bus and caravan but considering the two-hour drive there and back, plus the potential problems of people drinking and driving, that plan was nixed.

The event was kicked off that morning with local Fox affiliate KMSP-TV Channel 9 covering it live on its morning news program. Roving reporter M.A. Rosko was on the scene at the old bottling house, interviewing Ted and Jodi Marti, and yours truly, showing some pieces from my own Grain Belt memorabilia collection. The big event was scheduled to happen later that day, beginning at 5 p.m.

But a few short hours after the KMSP morning show signed off, a major news event broke. Senator Paul Wellstone, his wife, daughter and five others were killed in a small plane crash between campaign stops in northern Minnesota, days before the election. Schell management and

Moving party attendees were invited to sign the keg that would be used to transport the Grain Belt recipe to New Ulm.

party organizers called an emergency meeting to decide if the party should go on as planned. On one hand, hundreds of invited guests would be disappointed if turned away, but on the other, it could potentially become a public relations disaster if the media spin was "Sen. Wellstone died but Grain Belt went on with their party anyway." It was ultimately decided, however, that the party should go on.

Hundreds still showed up, but perhaps not as many as otherwise would have, which turned out to be a blessing in disguise as it had been over-booked with people who had signed up on the website. The Wellstone tragedy was talked about amongst the guests and while the room was undoubtedly filled with supporters and admirers of the late senator, a nice party might have been just what they needed at the moment.

Souvenir T-shirts were a popular item for sale, and I moved several copies of my 1998 book "Legend of the Brewery." Several local Grain Belt collectors including myself had displays of memorabilia, the polka band played, people lined up for the salty snacks and especially the free Grain Belt Premium beer. Guests signed the aluminum keg, and the recipe was dropped into it and sealed up, to cheers of delight. (The keg now resides in the Grain Belt wing of the Schell's Museum on the grounds of the brewery.)

The taps were shut off and the music stopped at 7 p.m. in order to keep things from going on too long and getting unruly. It was a fun party, if overshadowed by the events of the day.

Return of a Local Legend

The acquisition of Grain Belt brought big changes to the August Schell Brewing Company. While Schell's produced several different brews under its own name and under contract with others, Grain Belt Premium alone became the company's top selling brand within weeks of acquiring it. Annual production at Schell increased from 70,000 barrels per year before acquiring Grain Belt to 110,000 the year after and continued to increase in the ensuing years.

Schell had already been upgrading its facilities, building a new brewhouse alongside the old one in 1998, but the addition of Grain Belt necessitated further upgrades and expansion. New canning lines were put in to speed up production, more storage tanks were installed in the brewhouse, other equipment upgrades were made and the workforce at the New Ulm brewery was expanded. Soon, a new tour center was built on the brewery grounds, housing a gift shop, taproom and brewery museum filled with historic Schell's and Grain Belt artifacts.

Schell made the decision to limit the Grain Belt product line in the beginning to Grain Belt Premium and Premium Light. Original Golden Grain Belt was essentially forgotten, and talk of reviving the Grain Belt Archive Series never materialized. Product labels for Grain Belt Premium looked nearly identical to those used by Minnesota Brewing Company in the 1990s, with some minor changes to the bottles. Red and white were the colors for Premium, and blue and white were the colors for Premium Light.

August Schell Brewing Company invested over $1 million in marketing Grain Belt Premium as soon as it acquired the brand, teaming up with Minneapolis-based advertising agency Olson + Company to come up with campaigns that would emphasize the local heritage of the brand, while being relevant to contemporary consumers.

The company utilized the grainbelt.com website to add an element of fan participation to the marketing of the brand. Grain Belt Premium was promoted as a "Local Legend" and in early 2003 the company asked Grain Belt drinkers to nominate their own "local legends." Out of some 2,500 responses, the list was narrowed down to ten nominees, including retired AWA pro wrestler Baron von Raschke ("The Claw"); Wally the Beerman, a fixture at Twin Cities sporting events selling cold beer to fans, as well as in numerous local television commercials; and the Lake Mille Lacs walleye statue in Garrison, MN.

Subsequent audience-participation ad campaigns utilizing the Grain Belt website included a battle of the bands contest for local groups, and a Create Your Own Grain Belt Commercial contest, almost reminiscent of the Create Your Own Grain Belt Billboard contest back in

1973, but this time the entries were released to the public, many of which can still be seen on the website YouTube.

In the Twin Cities Metro Area, Grain Belt Premium sponsored lots of events popular with hip, young drinkers, including pub crawls, performances by local bands in area nightclubs, and for several years, birthday bashes for Minnesota Public Radio's pop music channel The Current.

The smug naysayers who insisted Grain Belt was dead and predicted the acquisition would sink the August Schell Brewing Company were proved dead wrong. Through the early decades of the 21st Century, the Grain Belt franchise brought immense success to the company, as the company gave Grain Belt its biggest marketing push since the days of the Minneapolis brewery, far more than Heileman or Minnesota Brewing ever dreamed of doing.

Grain Belt Nordeast

In the spring of 2010, more than seven years after Schell began marketing Grain Belt Premium and Premium Light, the company announced an all new product to the franchise called Grain Belt Nordeast, as a tribute by the New Ulm brewer to the Northeast Minneapolis neighborhood where the original Grain Belt brewery operated, often pronounced "Nordeast" by its older residents.

Grain Belt Nordeast was dark in color but light in taste. It was described by the company as an American amber lager with "a light maltiness and hop aroma with a mild bitterness. Smooth taste with an excellent drinkability," with a "slight caramel flavor." Nordeast came in clear bottles with the classic 1940s Grain Belt bottle cap logo on the label, similar to the big sign on Nicollet Island, on a dark green background.

Grain Belt Nordeast was released with great fanfare on April 6, 2010 with another VIP party at the old Grain Belt Brewery bottling house in Minneapolis. In celebration of the event, a World War II anti-aircraft searchlight illuminated the still dark Grain Belt bottle cap sign on Nicollet Island. The beer became available to the public the next morning at 7 a.m. at Surdyk's Liquor Store in Northeast Minneapolis, which opened an hour earlier than usual in anticipation of a big turnout of customers wanting to try the new brew.

Come they did, with a long line outside of Surdyk's, of customers waiting to get in early that morning. According to City Pages, "Some patrons carried more than four cases at a time, while others snapped pictures of themselves in front of the large Nordeast display showcased in the (appropriately) northeast corner of the store. Ted Marti, president of the August Schell Brewing Company, was on hand signing bottles and cases for patrons."

Within hours, Surdyk's, and other Northeast Minneapolis liquor stores and bars that had Nordeast available, were sold out. The situation put the 150-year-old August Schell Brewing Company in a predicament. The success of Grain Belt Nordeast, along with another brew introduced by the company called Schell's Hopfenmalz was so overwhelming, the New Ulm brewer could not keep up with the demand.

Ted Marti of the Schell Brewery released a statement addressing the situation in June:

I now want to discuss the bittersweet situation at the brewery. With success can come challenges when operating out of a 150-year-old brewery. One obstacle we are facing is capacity. Currently we have maxed out our tank space. Last Thursday we installed one 560 barrel tank and we have two 750 barrel tanks on order. The addition of these tanks will help increase our brewing capacity. However, due to the strict timeline of the brewing process, it will be another month before we can get the additional product to market. Although the tank will be incredibly effective in the long run, unfortunately it cannot assist in the immediate demand for our beers.

To help insure that we better meet the demand of all of our Schell and Grain Belt products, we have decided to temporarily limit the distribution of Grain Belt Nordeast. Effective immediately, Nordeast will only be available in the metro and New Ulm area, the immediate backyards of the former Grain Belt Brewery and August Schell Brewery. Once the new tanks are fully incorporated in the brewing rotation, we will better be able to meet the demand for Grain Belt Nordeast and expand distribution location to all areas.

We thank you for your understanding and patience during this time. Once again, thank you for your support while we continue to pursue every avenue to get our product to you as soon as possible.
Ein Prosit,
Ted Marti,
President, August Schell Brewing Co.

New Directions

In the first decade that Grain Belt Premium was made by August Schell Brewing Company, the product's appearance remained relatively unchanged since the late 1990s when it was still being produced by Minnesota Brewing Company. But the marketing started to move in a new direction beginning in 2012 when new 16-ounce cans for Grain Belt Premium with a vintage look were introduced, emphasizing "Grain Belt" rather than "Premium," and featuring a logo similar to the one used by Minneapolis Brewing Company in the early 1950s, with the Bavarian-style lettering on a red diamond, displayed vertically over a gold diamond-pattern background.

Later that year, organizers of the Zombie Pub Crawl, an annual event near Halloween where hundreds (if not thousands) of mostly young adults dressed in zombie makeup and costumes invade bars across the Minneapolis-St. Paul area, approached the Schell Brewery about designing a special beer can for the event. Poster artist David Witt was hired to create a 12-

The new "vintage" Grain Belt Premium 16 oz. can and its counterpart, "Brain Belt" Zombie Pub Crawl beer, introduced in 2012.

ounce can design that spoofed the new 16-ounce Grain Belt cans, featuring the name "Brain Belt." To those who were kids in the 1970s, it was reminiscent of the old Wacky Packages stickers that were popular at the time, spoofing various product labels.

Some 50,000 cans of "Brain Belt" were produced, showing up at area retailers in October 2012 and were well received by the "zombies" as well as the general public. In subsequent years, new versions of "Brain Belt" came out in conjunction with the event.

In April 2013, a new ad campaign for Grain Belt Premium with a social media tie-in was introduced. The new slogan was, "We are the American in American Lager," meant to stir feelings of pride and patriotism. The campaign highlighted new topics every month, inviting Grain Belt drinkers to post photos of themselves enjoying Grain Belt Premium while doing something that ties in with the current theme to the official Grain Belt Facebook page. The April theme was "restoration." According to a press release, "The winner's photo featuring their project, a Grain Belt product, name and hometown will be used in Grain Belt advertisements and marketing collateral. The winner will be mailed a large Marti family signed printed version of the ad."

The press release went on to say, "Grain Belt

From 2013: "We are the American in American Lager."
Image courtesy August Schell Brewing Co.

beer is a local legend. For more than 100 years, Grain Belt has been the beer that fathers have passed on to sons and friends have passed among each other at local bars and watering holes. It is a beer that spans generations, and unlike many of the American Lagers being made today, it is still proudly made in the USA. Everything from the barley, hops, bottles and beer labels can be traced to locations here. This tradition and steadfast loyalty is why Grain Belt has become legendary-both here and across America."

2014 was a pivotal year for Grain Belt. In May, the 12-ounce packages for Premium received a vintage makeover, going "back to the future" with bottle labels and cans looking strikingly similar to the award-winning designs the original brewery was using back in the early '50s. The trademark on all packages and advertising reverted to the logo with the Bohemian-style font. The new Grain Belt cans looked identical to the bright red 1955 model (with a blue version for Premium Light), with the only major differences being the new cans were all-aluminum rather than three-piece tin-plated steel, they had an easy-open stay-tab top, plus a mandatory government health warning (required since 1989). Similarly, the bottle labels took on a classic 1950s look, complete with foil labels.

The new look of Grain Belt Premium and Premium Light, along with an original 1955 steel flat-top can (center).

The new design extended to Grain Belt Premium, Premium Light and Nordeast (with a green diamond Grain Belt logo). Loyal fans of Nordeast, however, were not keen on the new design. The name "Nordeast" was de-emphasized, just as "Premium" was de-emphasized on the other packages, and the classic 1940s bottle cap logo similar to the Nicollet Island sign was gone. August Schell Brewing Company got the message, and soon the old label for Nordeast reappeared.

On July 8, 2014, Grain Belt Premium was honored at the US Open Beer Championship, winning a silver medal in the American Lager/Pilsner category. This award came two decades after winning a gold medal at the Great American Beer Festival, while being brewed in St. Paul by Minnesota Brewing Company.

The re-designed Grain Belt family. Red for Premium, Green for Nordeast, Blue for Premium Light.
Image courtesy August Schell Brewing Co.

And a new product, a blueberry-flavored lager called Grain Belt Blu, was made available on tap exclusively at the Schell's and Grain Belt booth at the ten-day Minnesota State Fair for the first time that year. Every day saw long lines of people waiting for the new brew, and it was tapped out before the fair was over.

August Schell further changed the marketing direction of the Grain Belt franchise in 2014, naming Minneapolis-based Colle+McVoy as the new advertising agency. Having Minneapolis advertising agencies handling the marketing of Grain Belt maintained the brand's close ties to that city. An August Schell official said the company was looking for a marketing partner that would "think out of the box."

Colle+McVoy put new emphasis on an old slogan, "The Friendly Beer," and kicked off its first campaign for Grain Belt with a 20-second "manifesto" video with the message, "Be nice to others. The end." Grain Belt

Vintage look with a slightly edgy message. "It's a nice day--Let's louse it up some way."
Image courtesy August Schell Brewing Co.

billboards, a favorite advertising medium of the original brewery, made a comeback around the Twin Cities with an eye-catching, vintage look, featuring various slogans playing off the "friendly" theme such as "Let's get friendly," "A good friend stays true" and "Make a friend tonight."

Grain Belt Premium football pack.
Image courtesy August Schell Brewing Co.

Football-themed marketing is commonplace in the beer business, but Grain Belt put a whole new spin on it in the fall of 2015 with football-themed 12-packs of bottles for Premium and Nordeast. A graphic of stitches replaced the Grain Belt name on the labels, making the familiar red diamond logo resemble a football. The 12-pack cartons came with games involving bottles and caps that could be played with friends, in a spirit of "Friendly Rivalry."

Lock & Dam

In the spring of 2016, August Schell introduced another new product to the Grain Belt line, called Grain Belt Lock & Dam, described as "a copper lager with a crisp flavor profile." Unlike other current Grain Belt products, Lock & Dam came in brown (or amber) bottles, as original Grain Belt used to. The name, like Nordeast, was intended to be a tribute to the original Grain Belt brewery in Minneapolis. A press release said it was "Inspired by the Mississippi River and the hard working lock & dam that powered the original Grain Belt brewery."

Grain Belt Lock & Dam was released in conjunction with even bigger news, the announcement that the August Schell Brewing Company, after years of negotiations, had purchased the iconic Nicollet Island Grain Belt Beer sign on the outskirts of downtown Minneapolis, along with the surrounding land, with plans to restore the lighting in time for Grain Belt's upcoming 125th anniversary. Schell teamed up with historical consultants Hess, Roise and Company, which had also consulted the historic renovation of

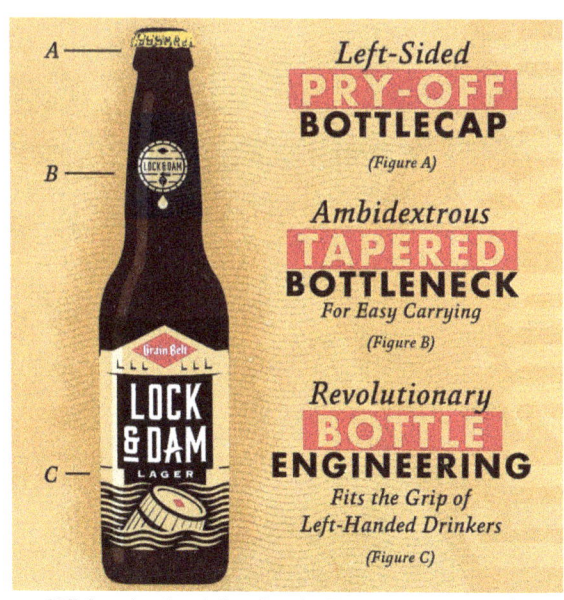

Whimsical ad for Grain Belt Lock & Dam.
Image courtesy August Schell Brewing Company

the old Grain Belt brewery, in getting the sign registered to the National Register of Historic Places.

Much would have to be done in restoring the old electric sign. Permits and paperwork from the City of Minneapolis would have to be filed and approved, a contractor would have to be found that could retrofit it with energy-efficient LEDs rather than going back to neon tubing and incandescent light bulbs, and funding would also have to be found for this very expensive project.

Re-lighting the big bottle cap

In late 2017, August Schell Brewing Company announced the long-awaited re-lighting of the landmark Grain Belt bottle cap sign on Nicollet Island in Minneapolis would finally happen. The project would be financed in part through the sale to the public of individual light bulbs in the sign's lettering for $100 each. The company quickly sold 1,007 "light bulb" packages that included a certificate of light bulb ownership, a T-shirt and a replica sign, according to an article

The Nicollet Island bottle cap sign, pictured in 2018.

in City Pages.

On December 30, 2017 at 5:30 p.m., thousands of hearty Minnesotans braved double-digit below zero winter temperatures to watch the big sign come back to life for the first time in more than two decades, flashing brighter than ever before with new LED technology. (On a personal note, I had to see it on TV in a hospital room, groggy from medication, with a serious case of flu and pneumonia.)

"The Grain Belt Beer sign has been present in the Minneapolis community since 1941 and has recently been named to the National Register of Historic Places," said Ted Marti of August Schell Brewing Company in a press release. "A family tradition since 1860, our historic Minnesota brewery is continually committed to preserving history, both at the brewery and in our community."

Following the re-lighting ceremony, an "After Glow" party was thrown at the nearby Nicollet Island pavilion, featuring local bands, and plenty of Grain Belt Premium. Tickets had to be purchased for the party, and it was naturally a 21-plus event.

Using LED lighting had many advantages. The sign burned brighter yet used far less energy, there was less need of repairs, and the colors could be changed with a flip of a switch. This was demonstrated a few weeks later as the Minnesota Vikings made it into the NFL playoffs, and the big sign was lit up in purple and gold. In later months, it was lit in red, white and blue for Independence Day, and in red and green for Christmas.

Grain Belt 125

The re-lighting of the Nicollet Island bottle cap sign kicked off a year-long celebration by August Schell Brewing Company of Grain Belt's 125th Anniversary in 2018. From the brand's introduction in 1893, its survival was pretty amazing, considering the fact that it always remained a regional product, and all the times it came close to death; Prohibition in 1920, attempts by old prohibitionists to snuff it out again after repeal, Irwin Jacobs and the closing of the original Minneapolis brewery in 1975, G. Heileman's ownership and indifference, corporate raider Alan Bond in 1987, and the sudden demise of Minnesota Brewing Company in 2002.

The anniversary was promoted with a series of six "throwback" commemorative Grain Belt bottle labels, introduced one at a time every two months through the course of the year, on bottles of Grain Belt Premium. The first replica label resembled the circa 1955 label that the company was already using on its cans, but subsequent labels in the series included designs from the 1930s and '40s, plus one pre-Prohibition label. The replica labels included the addition of the "Premium" logo that didn't originally appear, plus various modern-day mandatories such as bar codes, government health warnings and state deposit information.

When all six "throwback" labels were released, the company, by popular demand, produced a poster featuring the entire collection, with an image of the Minneapolis skyline in the background.

New Generation Products

In the spring of 2018, Grain Belt Blu blueberry flavored lager "made with real blueberry juice," an exclusive at the Minnesota State Fair since 2014, was introduced in cans (although not in bottles, where one could see the deep purple color of the brew) as a seasonal product. There were those who complained that Blu was a drastic step away from the original heritage of Grain Belt, but the sweet-tasting beer built a loyal following through

A poster issued by the Schell's Brewery featured all six of the Grain Belt commemorative labels, based on designs from the first half of the 20th Century.

Image courtesy August Schell Brewing Company.

Seasonal flavored beers are the latest products in the Grain Belt line.

Cerveza image courtesy August Schell Brewing Co.

the summer of 2018, and many were disappointed when it was discontinued in the fall and that they would have to wait until the following spring to enjoy it again.

Blu did come back in the spring of 2019, and another seasonal, Grain Belt Southwest Cerveza "Mexican-style lager with natural lime flavor" (a real drastic step away from the original heritage of Grain Belt), was introduced in cans. The colorful cans featured the slogan "We are simpatico!" Meanwhile, original Golden Grain Belt remained in the ash heep of history.

With several different brews now being made under the Grain Belt brand, brewed for contemporary tastes, it's not really the same Grain Belt as it was before. Some Grain Belt fans of old are perplexed by some of the current marketing. But the heritage lives on. One can only speculate on what the likes of Frank Kiewel or Jacob Kunz, or for that matter John Orth would think of Grain Belt in the 21st Century.

From "The Heritage of America's Grain Belt" (1952).

History of Grain Belt

Historically, John Orth was the first brewer to arrive during 1850 in what was to become Minneapolis. He settled here and opened the first brewery located on the site where the Grain Belt Brewery stands today.

Other brewing minded business men were later attracted to Minneapolis and opened their own brewing operations. Among these were: The Heinrich Brewing Association, F. D. Norenberg Brewery and Malt House, and the Germania Brewing Company. These companies ultimately merged with the Orth Brewing Company in 1891 under the name Minneapolis Brewing and Malting Company. In 1893 this company became the Minneapolis Brewing Company and introduced Grain Belt Beer.

**GRAIN BELT
OLD BOTTLE COLLECTION**

In 1920, Congress enacted prohibition forcing all brewing operations out of the alcoholic beer business. To survive this era from 1920 to 1933, Minneapolis Brewing Company produced and bottled "Near Beer" and soft drinks. In 1933 prohibition was repealed enabling the reorganization and production of Grain Belt products. In 1967 the Company's name was changed to Grain Belt Breweries, Inc.

The Company has enjoyed steady growth in sales and marketing area, broadening from the Upper Peninsula of Michigan across the northern tier of states to the Pacific Coast and then south as far as Texas and Arizona. The prime marketing areas are Minnesota, North Dakota, South Dakota, Iowa, Wisconsin, and Nebraska. Grain Belt ranks as the 18th largest brewery in the United States.

Grain Belt, located at 1215 Marshall Street N. E., is the only brewery in Minneapolis and is the only locally owned brewery in the Twin Cities.

In addition to Grain Belt products, the Company has during the past 15 years produced and marketed White Label, Hauenstein, and Storz beers.

Grain Belt is a publicly owned company having over 2,000 stockholders with its shares listed on the Midwest Stock Exchange.

We sincerely hope that you find this brochure interesting and informative. We enjoyed having you as our guests and hope you will join us again in the near future. You are always welcome at Grain Belt.

30 Years ago at Grain Belt

	1973	1943
SALES	$34 MILLION	$8 MILLION
PAYROLLS AND BENEFITS	$7 MILLION	$1 MILLION

Grain Belt pays annual taxes totaling $12 million including excise, income, property, sales, and payroll taxes.

Welcome to Grain Belt®

History of beer

The history of beer is almost as old as the known history of mankind. Mention is made of cereal beverages in records of the nations of Asia, hundreds of years before the Christian Era. The cultivation of barley and making of malt are believed to have originated in Egypt. The Chinese, Egyptians, Greeks, and Romans brewed beer.

There are some "beer historians" who claim that Noah had beer with him when he set sail in the Ark. Four kinds of beer were known in the land of the Nile about 3,000 B. C. Herodotus, writing in the fourth century, describes the barley beverage as the popular drink of Egypt. A barley beverage is mentioned in the "Book of the Dead", a record of the ancient Egyptian kings which scholars say is 5,000 years old.

Beer was used for hundreds of years on sailing vessels to prevent scurvy and to keep the crew in "good spirits." In 1445 a charter was granted in England to a Brewer's Guild. The Pilgrims had beer on the Mayflower. Women brewed most of the beer in the early days. During the Middle Ages, brewhouses were established in monasteries and villages.

The art of brewing beer has been of constantly growing importance for more than a thousand years. Materials and methods differed from country to country, but the use of cereals instead of fruit is the link which brings all of the early cereal beverages under the classification of "beers."

Brewing of Grain Belt

The ingredients in Grain Belt Beer are selected barley malt, corn, hops, the finest diamond clear brewing water and brewers yeast. Barley malt is the basic material of beer, providing body and flavor. Processed corn aids the lightness of beer, while domestic and imported hops provide the proper seasoning. Our strain of yeast ferments the product and assures uniformity, brew after brew. Our diamond clear, perfect brewing water comes from wells reaching the Hinckley vein 1,075 feet deep.

MASH TANK — Barley malt, processed corn and our diamond clear brewing water are heated for two hours at 165° F. in the mash tank at which time the starches are converted to fermentable sugars. At this stage of the brewing process the mixture is called wort.

STRAINMASTER — The wort is then clarified, strained through the fine screens of our strainmaster, and transferred to the brew kettle. The spent barley grains remaining are removed, dried, and sold for cattle feed.

BREW KETTLE — In the copper brew kettle our diamond clear brewing water is added to the wort on a precise time schedule, then cooked at the 212° F. boiling point for over two hours. At specified times our select hops are added for proper seasoning.

FERMENTER — The wort then leaves the kettle, is filtered, quickly cooled to 48° F., brewers yeast is added, and then transferred to a large fermenting tank. During the long fermenting process the action of the yeast achieves proper alcoholic strength and upon completion the product now becomes beer.

AGING TANK — The beer then goes through several stages in the aging process, is filtered to brilliance, and properly carbonated. Thorough checks are made by our Quality Control Laboratory prior and during the time our beer is packaged in kegs, cans, and bottles.

Now you have Grain Belt Beer. A combination of the finest ingredients available with delicate, skilled processing in our historic, yet modern, Brewery.

The Best things in Life Are Here!

Been a long time a-brewing

**BREWERS OF:
Golden Grain Belt,
Grain Belt Premium,
White Label,
Hauenstein
and Storz Beers.**

Tour Schedules

June — September, 9:00 — 11:00 a. m. and 1:00 — 3:00 p. m. every half hour Monday thru Friday; October — May, 10:00 a. m., 1:00 p. m., and 2:00 p. m. Monday thru Friday.

1974 Grain Belt tour brochure.

About the author

Jeff R. Lonto, author of "Diamond Clear—Friendly Beer, the Grain Belt Story."

Jeff R. Lonto has been a connoisseur of all things Grain Belt since long before he was old enough to legally buy it. In 1993 he moved into the Minneapolis neighborhood of the old Grain Belt brewery, which had closed nearly two decades earlier. He started Studio Z-7 Publishing in 1997 and published his first book, "Fiasco At 1280-- The Rise and Hard Fall of a Twin Cities Radio Station" in 1998, followed by his first Grain Belt history, "Legend of the Brewery--A Brief History of the Minneapolis Brewing Heritage." Since then he has published several books and articles on a range of topics, and he is a board member and the newsletter editor for the North Star Chapter Breweriana Club.

STUDIO Z·7
PUBLISHING
INDEPENDENT PUBLISHING SINCE 1997

Pop History...from a Creative Perspective.

1927 trade poster.

Studio Z-7 Publishing is a media resource that specializes in history and popular culture. In the coming year we are publishing new books which can be found on our website (www.studioz7.com) along with free-to-read articles and essays focusing on 1960s and '70s pop culture.

News from the Studio can be found on our Facebook page (facebook.com/studioz7pub) along with some nostalgic nuggets from our archive.

Studio Z-7 video projects plus vintage TV commercials and radio airchecks can be found on our YouTube page (youtube.com/user/StudioZ7). Audiobooks, radio interviews, etc. can be found on our SoundCloud page (soundcloud.com/studio-z-7-publishing).

Jeff and Jill of the staff.

Studio Z-7 Publishing is based in an area of Minneapolis known as the Northeast Arts District, since 1997.

www.studioz7.com

www.ingramcontent.com/pod-product-compliance
Lightning Source LLC
Chambersburg PA
CBHW061210230426
43665CB00028B/2968